THE WORST FOOTBALL KITS

OF ALL TIME

The Worst Football Kits of All Time

Dave Moor

This work is dedicated to my family who have variously tolerated or encouraged my obsessive interest in the history of football strips and above all to my dad, the late Kenneth Moor, whose chance remark to an impressionable 13-year-old in July 1966 set the ball rolling

First published 2011

The History Press
The Mill, Brimscombe Port
Stroud, Gloucestershire, GL5 2QG
www.thehistorypress.co.uk

British Library Cataloguing in Publication Data.
A catalogue record for this book is available from the British
Library.

ISBN 978 0 7524 5904 2

Typesetting and origination by The History Press
Production managed by Jellyfish Print Solutions and manufactured in India

CONTENTS

FOREWORD

Only eight years separated the publication of my book *Club Colours* and the appearance of Dave's wonderful website, historicalkits.co.uk. However, in that time the interest in the sartorial elegance (or not) of football teams was in the process of undergoing a great boom. Gone are the days when that interest was the domain solely of a few passionate nerds who would have been amazed to discover the existence of like-minded fanatics.

Back in the 1950s, these characters relied on the pre-season annuals such as *Playfair* and *News of the World* for news of changes, often using the vocabulary of 'jerseys' and 'knickers' – or more often had to resort to direct observation at matches. Indeed, I was lucky enough to support Crewe Alexandra whose team was so inept that it enabled me to quiz the opposing goalkeepers about recent kit changes – such was the one-sided nature of most games!

By the 1960s, at which time I was working in central London, not only were there more UK football magazines with lots of photographs, but one could also find exotic delights as *Kicker Sport* and *Nepes Sports*. These were to widen interest to a huge international level.

At about the same time, evidence of other afflicted souls came to light in the personal pages of *World Soccer*, etc. Letters were sent, information swapped (often badly drawn) and friendships formed, but progress was slow. Snatched meetings around the country followed (one such abortive attempt occurred when I and a fellow collector sat in different pubs of the same name in neighbouring villages with virtually the same name for several hours – we never met!) but it was not until the arrival of the internet that our interest was to remain anything other than very inefficient.

At the same time, the kits themselves were becoming more important. Materials were more sympathetic to detail and the fans themselves showed greater interest. Indeed, eventually, the efforts of the new nerds who would wear their own homemade imitation shirts, were superseded by the market-aware manufacturing of millions of official – and accurate – replica shirts.

But again, there were more twists in the tale. The newly aware fans gradually overcame their blind, uncritical allegiances and murmurs of unappreciated and positively hated versions of honoured shirts emerged. Away strips bore the brunt of this unhappiness. As the clubs and their kit manufacturers sought bigger market sales, many of these new designs were aimed solely at High Street wear – and even as 'holiday uniforms' – and of course, were not to everyone's tastes.

Eventually, some of the shirts were to become infamous and a new fight between 'collectors' and 'iconoclasts' began – but that is Dave's story to tell.

Bob Bickerton

INTRODUCTION

I n 1973 Admiral Sportswear reinvented football strips in order to sell cheap nylon replicas to the parents of eager schoolboys at premium prices. From these small beginnings a multi-million pound global market has developed and fans eagerly anticipate each season's new offerings.

An important part of this annual ritual is the debate on how the new strip measures up to previous versions. Invariably the discussion includes heated exchanges about the best and worst kits worn by the club in question. There is no definition of what makes a bad kit. A decent design may be tainted by failure on the pitch or misconduct in the boardroom. Equally an ugly outfit may become popular if it is associated with success. Attempts to reinvent a club's image by introducing a novel colour scheme will be met with acclaim if the team wins something, derision if they fail.

Furthermore, nostalgia is an important factor. Shirts reviled in the 1970s and '80s are now highly collectible. Few shirts from earlier periods have survived because in those days they were handed down to the reserves and then to the juniors until they

literally fell apart. Genuine match-worn shirts from the 1960s and earlier are as rare as hen's teeth and command prices at auction to match.

This phenomenon has generated considerable interest in the history of club kits and their associated heritage, which opens up the fascinating evolution of football kits from the 1860s to the present day.

Organised football evolved in English public schools in the nineteenth century. When these young gentlemen went up to university or joined the Army, many wanted to continue to play football but as each school had its own code, attempts to stage games descended into chaos. The first set of uniform rules were drawn up at Cambridge University in 1848. In 1857 the world's first football club, Sheffield FC, set out what became known as the Sheffield Rules, adopted by newly emerging clubs throughout the Midlands. The Football Association was formed in 1863 and for a time the FA and Sheffield Rules coexisted until a single set was agreed in 1877.

During this formative period, games were normally played between scratch teams from the same club: married men v bachelors, tradesmen v professions and so forth. Players turned out in whatever kit they had to hand and teams were distinguished by wearing distinctive headgear, scarves and/or sashes.

The inauguration of the FA Cup in 1872 encouraged a trend for inter-club matches and teams began to introduce distinctive colours, but this was not universally adopted. In 1879 a correspondent wrote to a Birmingham newspaper:

> In football it is a most essential point that the members of one team should be clearly distinguished from those of the other. The only way this can be effected is for each club to have a distinct uniform as the diversity of dress displayed yesterday not only confused the members of the team but the spectators [who] were quite unable to say whether a man belonged to one team or the other.

The teams that emerged in the 1870s were rooted in the public school system so it is no surprise that many of them took their often extravagant and highly individual colours from these institutions. Members had to provide their own kit, which was not a problem for the wealthy gentlemen-players of the period who could place an order with their tailor, but there was little standardisation. Early photographs of the Wednesday and Stoke, for example, reveal considerable variations between individual players' tops.

In the 1880s a new breed of club emerged in the north and Midlands of England and the central belt of Scotland as labour reforms provided the working class with a degree of leisure time. These clubs were run by hard-nosed businessmen in pursuit of profit and drew their players as well as supporters from local factories, pits and mills.

As the new working class clubs eclipsed the old elite, the extravagant colours of the latter were gradually replaced by simpler designs that were more affordable. Whereas the old-school teams regarded spectators as a nuisance, the new clubs built enclosed grounds to extract entrance fees. As attendances grew it became increasingly important that spectators could make out their team's players at a distance. This fed a trend for simpler shirts in bold colours, which could be mass-produced at affordable prices by emerging sportswear manufacturers such as Bukta (founded 1879) and Umbro (1910).

After the turn of the twentieth century, football strips became generally, well, sensible. Vertical stripes and horizontal hoops became broader: much easier to see on a murky November afternoon. As the century progressed, kits evolved gradually. Laced crew necks were popular for a while but were progressively replaced with collared shirts while knickers became baggier. In 1954 the first lightweight 'continental style' strips were introduced by Umbro, featuring short sleeves and V-necks as well as shorter shorts and a decade later, crew necks, skimpy shorts and lightweight socks were all the rage.

The designs that accompanied this gradual evolution in the manufacture of football strips remained solidly conservative, which is why there are so few entries in this volume between

1900 and 1980. It was the introduction of polyester as the fabric of choice in the mid-1980s that led to a design revolution and the style calamity of the mid-1990s. Unlike cotton, polyester could be printed using a novel process of dye sublimation, which allowed complex patterns and design effects (such as the shadow stripes worn by Spurs in the 1982 FA Cup final) to be heat printed directly onto the fabric.

As the market for replica shirts expanded, design became focussed on the leisurewear market, increasingly dominated by demand for branded sportswear such as trainers, tracksuits and the abominable shell-suit. To compete, designers introduced extravagant designs and novel colours (who can forget the grey, teal and ecru outfits of the period?).

Inevitably, perhaps, the pendulum of fashion has since swung in the opposite direction, Nike leading the way in producing minimalist strips as the millennium approached. Forward-thinking clubs began to consult with fans before introducing new strips and their vote was consistently in favour of traditional designs, albeit with modern flourishes.

Overall the design of football strips has improved considerably over the last decade while the proliferation of anniversaries has led clubs to look back over their kit heritage to produce some fine designs inspired by the past. On the debit side, too many clubs now introduce at least one set of new shirts each season not to mention spurious third kits, treating loyal supporters as cash cows rather than valued customers.

In putting together this volume, I would like to say that I have sought to represent a general consensus of opinion. This would be untrue. While I have included comments from committed collectors, historians and supporters, in the final analysis this is my own biased, subjective and somewhat partisan selection. Sorry about that. I have also introduced some oddities from the Victorian and later eras that are, to say the least, obscure. The focus is firmly on English and Scottish clubs but a few noteworthy specimens from the rest of the world are included just for fun.

Enjoy.

Dave Moor,
South Wales, 2011

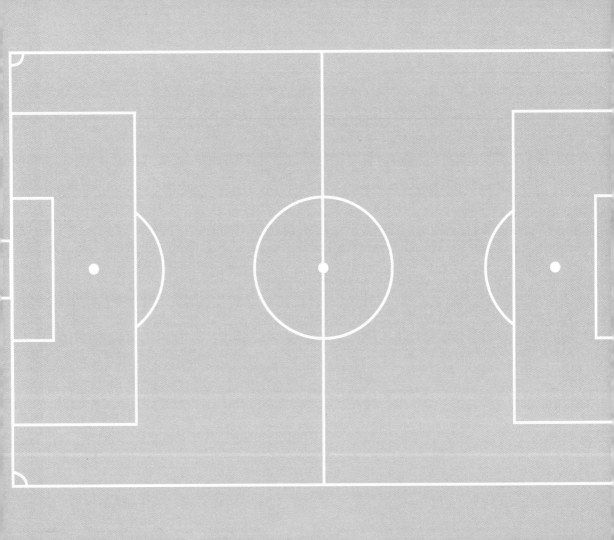

1ST LANARKSHIRE VOLUNTEER RIFLES 1874

In 1859 the Secretary of State for War, Jonathan Peel, authorised the formation of volunteer rifle corps throughout the UK to form a local defence force in time of war. After 1872 these volunteer units, originally under the command of Lord Lieutenants in the counties, were increasingly integrated into the regular Army. A great many of these volunteer rifle regiments in Scotland formed football sections as a way of attracting working-class recruits and providing healthy, competitive exercise, thus playing an important role in the spread of the game in Scotland.

1st Lanarkshire VR's astonishingly dull strip was not unusual for the period inasmuch as it was not intended to allow spectators to distinguish their team from opponents. At this time, spectators were regarded as a nuisance.

10TH LANARKSHIRE VOLUNTEERS 1884–5

After 1881 the volunteer rifle corps were integrated into new county infantry regiments consisting of regular, militia and volunteer battalions, supervised by regular Army officers. Over 90 volunteer battalions registered football sections with the Scottish FA between 1875 and 1900.

Based in Glasgow between 1884 and 1886, 10th Lanarkshire RV wore conventional navy jerseys, red hose and knickerbockers made up from Black Watch tartan, presumably because they were associated with the Royal Highland Regiment (the Black Watch).

 ## ABERDEEN 1994–5

'Since 1939 Aberdeen's kits have been red with varying amounts of white trim but for some reason this strip had blue paint splashes all over the top and shorts. Fans even started a campaign to get the blue removed. Thankfully the kits went back to red and white the following season.'

STUART STEPHEN – Aberdeen supporter

👉 © Offside

 ## ABERDEEN AWAY 1995–7

'This was an absolutely disastrous design effort, even for its time. It's known among Dons fans as the (ahem) "vomit top". Draw your own conclusions . . .'

STEVE TURNER – Aberdeen supporter

👉 © Offside

AIRDRIEONIANS 1992-3

Airdrie started to wear all-white with a red chevron on the shirt in 1912, based on the design worn by Manchester United in the FA Cup final of 1909. The V was repeated on the back giving rise to their popular nickname of 'the Diamonds'. A link up with Hummel in 1992 might have worked out well, given that the Danish company's trademark chevrons were not a million miles from Airdrie's treasured design. The result was, unfortunately, a bit of a shocker. The V was reduced to a shadow of its former glory, peeking shyly out from beneath the collar while the shirt itself was dominated by grotesque grey patterns based on diamonds and chevrons in disturbing abstract patterns.

☞ www.classicfootballshirts.co.uk

AJAX AMSTERDAM AWAY 1989-90

Ajax are famous for Johann Cruyff, total football and their iconic white strip with a broad red stripe down the shirt front. For the 1989–90 season, when colours clashed, Bergkamp, Van 't Schip and Mühren turned out in this horrid shirt designed by Umbro, with a complex geometric design superimposed on a plain blue background with fashionable pinstripes. This appalling top laid down a benchmark that Umbro and its competitors sought to exceed for sheer bad taste over the following decade.

☞ www.classicfootballshirts.co.uk

ALDENHAM SCHOOL 1870

The modern game emerged from the various forms of football played in England's public schools, each of which had their own rules. In these institutions brutality was considered character-building, a value reflected in the rules which permitted charging opponents, gouging and hacking (deliberately kicking an opponent's shins in order to bring him down). Aldenham School were among the first to codify their rules in 1825. Since no one else played by the same code, matches were confined to inter-house competition but by 1870, several schools organised annual games against old boys' XIs. Aldenham wore plain white, embellished with black turbans in these games. Yes, I did say turbans.

ARSENAL AWAY 1982-3

In fashion circles the phrase 'blue and green should never be seen without something in between' is a given. Trinny and Susannah may take issue with this but back in 1982, Arsenal's decision to drop their famous yellow and blue change strip in favour of this ensemble did not meet with general approval and it was quietly dropped after just one season.

☞ www.oldfootballshirts.com

ARBROATH WANDERERS 1892-4

Formed in 1892, Arbroath Wanderers existed for just six seasons before they disappeared. Their colours were recorded with the Scottish Football Association as 'red, blue and chocolate'. The graphic shows the most likely configuration.

ARSENAL AWAY 1991-3

The outbreak of good taste at Highbury in 1983 lasted just eight seasons before Adidas and Arsenal unleashed the infamous 'bruised banana' on an unsuspecting public. The yellow shirt was now disfigured by an inexplicable pattern of navy chevrons while the red trim provided a jarring counterpoint. Replicas of this shirt, which features in most punters' top ten of kit horrors, now change hands for considerable sums, which goes to prove that given time, even the worst designs can become desirable.

☞ Ian Wright checks he has all of his equipment. © Offside

ASTON VILLA 1885-6

Villa are associated with their iconic claret jerseys and light blue sleeves, designed for the club by Ollie Whateley, who played for Villa and England in the 1890s and who was a graphic designer by trade. Prior to this the club wore all sorts of colours and research by Bernard Gallagher has uncovered references to the team wearing 'piebald' tops. Sadly no photographic evidence of these remarkable jerseys survives so our graphic represents a best guess at what they looked like.

ASTON VILLA AWAY 1993-5

In 1993 Villa signed up with Asics who provided the club with a novel home strip in a sort of purple-claret shade with narrow blue stripes. Not too popular perhaps, but a design that did have resonance with some Villa shirts from the Victorian era. The same could not be said for the away kit in green, black and red, a combination designed to strike horror into the observer. As with so many shirt atrocities of the period, these are now collectors' items but that does not make it good.

☞ Martin Keown is quite happy to stay away from that kit, but there's no escaping it for John Fashanu. © Offside

ATHLETIC BILBAO 2004-5

Athletic Bilbao are proud of their cultural heritage and to this day will only engage players born in the Basque territory. The club's English prefix is a reminder of their original founders, British steelworkers who worked in Bilbao's shipyards and local students returning from the UK. Since 1910 the team has played in red and white stripes, possibly inspired by English teams from Southampton or Sunderland where some of the British founders originated, or more likely because local mills had cloth left over from making mattress covers.

To mark their centenary in 2004 local artist Dario Urzay was commissioned to produce a special shirt. Taking his inspiration from pieces in the Bilbao Guggenheim Museum, Urzay came up with this astonishing design, which was worn only in the UEFA Cup before being retired. It is believed that an example can now be found in the Salvador Dali Museum, where it will be completely at home.

AUSTRALIA 1991

On 19 April 1984, Sir Ninian Stephen, then Governor-General of Australia, proclaimed that the green and gold traditionally worn by all Australian national sporting teams would henceforth be *the* official national colours. I'm not sure what Sir Ninian would have thought of this effort.

☞ A brilliant Technicolor yawn from Down Under.
www.oldfootballshirts.com

FK AUSTRIA VIENNA 1990–1

At the time the Austrian football authorities permitted clubs to sell naming rights to sponsors so the club's official title was Austria Memphis. In this instance and despite mounting pressure from government and health organisations, the sponsor was a tobacco company, a long-standing sponsorship deal that did not end until 2004.

Adidas produced this design for the club with what appear to be delicate wisps of smoke wafting across the top of the shirt.

☞ www.oldfootballshirts.com

 ## BALGAY 1880–1

A Dundee side that existed for just four short seasons, their colours were registered with the Scottish FA as 'maroon and drab'. This may have been just a bit too colourful, so in their final season they played in black jerseys.

 ## ACEC BARAÚNAS OF MOSSORÓ (v ES PAUFERRENSE) 1997–8

'Once upon a time, football teams would choose strips to distinguish their players from their opponents and allow their supporters to pick out individuals during the progress of a match. However, as the popularity of the game has grown at an increasingly accelerated pace in recent years, commercial interests seem to have outgrown much of the early simple reasoning of the sport.

'Not only was this a problem in the commercially sophisticated competitions of Europe. In Brazil this phenomenon permeated even to clubs in the lower regional state leagues. One typical such team was ACEC Baraúnas of Mossoró in Rio Grande de Norte. The club's traditional colours of red, white and green – most likely influenced by those of Fluminense of Rio and also those of Portugal – once simple, had become increasingly modernised vertical stripes, further cross-sectioned diagonally with the resulting "diamond" facets then irregularly coloured in a random format.

'The end result became a kind of jungle camouflage, and of course, its ease of recognition was further diminished as the shirts had to stand out of a background of verdant turf, white lines and the often exposed patches of tropical red earth. Matters would become worse when Baraúnas played against teams such as ES Pauferrense whose yellow, blue, green and white ensemble was equally confusing.

'Obviously, spectators were being treated to some advanced eye test and hopefully, at least had a distinctive ball to follow. Why club officials should risk the discontent of players and fans, merely to follow "modern" trends is anyone's guess!'

BOB BICKERTON

☞ Bob Bickerton

 # BARNET 1888-98

The early history of the modern Barnet FC is a tangled affair but research by Tony Rayner and Steve Wilmott has revealed that the original Barnet club was formed in 1885 as New Barnet FC. Players who failed to turn up in the official colours of black shirts, socks and caps with white knickerbockers were liable to a fine of 6*d*. In 1888 the club became known simply as Barnet FC and adopted pale violet and black shirts. The club folded in 1901 after they were suspended by the FA for breach of the rules on amateurism that applied at the time.

 # BARNSLEY ST PETER'S 1889-91

In the 1880s labour reforms meant that most working people were no longer required to work on Saturday afternoons but there was little to do by way of recreation aside from drinking in public houses. Many clergymen in this era of muscular Christianity saw Association Football as a healthy alternative that offered parishioners exercise in the open air as well as companionship. In fact a great many English clubs owe their origins to the pastoral motives of local clergy: think of Southampton, Everton, Manchester City, Mansfield Town and Bolton Wanderers to name but a few, all of whom were originally attached to local churches or chapels.

Barnsley were founded by the splendidly named the Revd Tiverton Preedy and until 1897 included the name of their founders' church in their title. This idiosyncratic strip, adopted in 1889 combines vertical stripes on the body with horizontal ones on the sleeves.

 **BARNSLEY 1989-90**

'Tonight, Matthew, I'm going to be
Paul Cross of Barnsley.' © Offside

Barnsley have played in sober red shirts and white shorts since 1898, 'nowt fancy sithee'. This unique 'star-strip' appeared in 1989 and broke the mould completely. It disappeared the following season.

BIRMINGHAM CITY AWAY 1970s

In the early 1970s Birmingham City, with Trevor Francis in the ranks, enjoyed something of a renaissance even though they did not win anything. This was the period of the fondly remembered 'penguin strip' consisting of royal blue shirts with a broad white panel on the front of the shirts. City's normal change kit was similar but in red and white but for some games they turned out in this splendid recreation of the flag of West Germany. 'Brummagem über alles' and all that.

Male model and professional footballer for famous West Midlands club are just two careers your humble author has NOT followed.

BIRMINGHAM CITY 1992-3

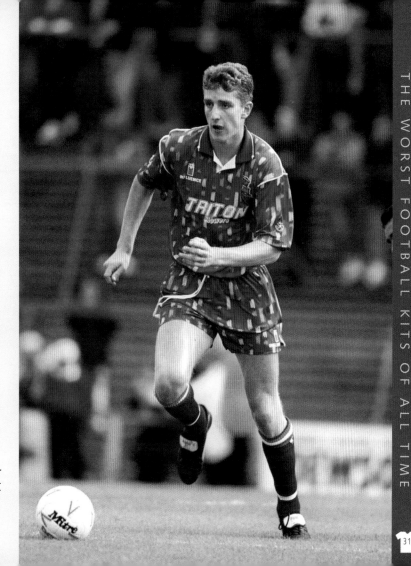

In April 1989 the Kumar brothers, owners of a local clothing chain, bought a controlling interest in the club, which was then languishing in Division Three. Under their own Influence brand, the Kumars began to provide the club's kits in 1991. This effort from 1992, with splotches of green, yellow and dark blue marks a low point in the club's kit history. The orange, white and green stocking trim represents the brothers' Indian associations. When the Kumars' business empire collapsed, the club was taken over by David Sullivan of Sports Newspapers and this unpopular strip was replaced before the season finished.

'I can't think why you've selected this kit – it's such a lovely ensemble!'

PETER LEWIS, Club Editor
Birmingham City FC

☞ Birmingham City FC

BIRKIRKARA
1999-2000

In the modest world of Maltese professional football, Birkirkara FC, who play in one of the island's largest towns, are a force to be reckoned with, having won the Maltese Premier League three times, most recently in 2009/10. Their red and yellow colours made them a natural partner for Ronald McDonald a decade ago.

Maltese McFootball shirt.
www.oldfootballshirts.com

VFL BOCHUM
1997-8

Bochum have a history that goes back to 1848 when they were formed as a gymnastics club. Throughout Germany's turbulent history the club survived bans and state-enforced mergers and when the Bundesliga was formed in 1963, they were placed in the third tier Amateurliga Westfalen from which they rose steadily into the Bundesliga in 1971. Since then they have regularly moved between the first and second tiers. The club's usual colours are blue and white but in 1997 extraordinary rainbow bands augmented their shirts.

Sergei Yuran is somewhere over the rainbow. © Offside

BOLTON WANDERERS 1884-5

Clubs changed colours with some frequency in the Victorian period, depending on what could be obtained from local suppliers. In the days before professionalism was recognised it was the responsibility of the players to buy their own kit and it appears that one local gents' outfitter may have had a job lot of white cotton with red spots. Sadly, no photographs of this remarkable outfit survive, although we do have reliable contemporary references from the local press, so our graphic represents our interpretation of this extraordinary outfit.

BORUSSIA DORTMUND 1999-2000

Compared to their usual acid-yellow outfits, this shirt was positively mellow. The problem arose when a German consumer affairs programme, *Plusminus*, discovered that the shirts contained traces of TBT (tribultytin) to reduce odour from excessive sweating. TBT is also used in anti-barnacle paint to protect ships and is highly poisonous. Sales of replica shirts were suspended although Nike insisted, 'Small doses of TBT when used in textiles are not normally dangerous to humans.' The team played out the season in the toxic tops without suffering any ill-effects and remain, as far as we know, completely free of barnacles.

☞ Dortmund's toxic top. www.oldfootballshirts.com

AFC BOURNEMOUTH AWAY 1992-3

BRADFORD CITY 1923-4

'"Everything," replied Tony Pulis when asked to register the details of Bournemouth's away colours for the 1992/93 season. This lime, lilac, white and chocolate zig-zag affair sent the eyes into disbelief. The shirt reflected the season's performances – dire.'

GAVIN MEADEN,
Cherries supporter

 www.oldfootballshirts.com

This interesting example underlines the historical relationship that both Bradford clubs have with the Rugby League code that remains important in the city and from which both the City and Park Avenue clubs were formed. The double chevron is a style distinctly associated with professional rugby rather than soccer.

BRADFORD CITY 1991-2

Throughout their history, the Bantams have worn distinctive colours of claret, amber and black, a combination unique in the Football League. Furthermore, the club has never been afraid to experiment with novel arrangements: the claret jerseys with amber yoke worn in the 1911 FA Cup final are a design classic while the striped shirts worn with black shorts adopted in the late 1960s have become their signature strip. It is, however, hard to find words to describe some of the awful designs they adopted in the early 1990s, of which this is certainly the worst.

 www.oldfootballshirts.com

BRENTFORD 1889–90

Brentford FC were formed as an offshoot of the Brentford Rowing Club, adopting the association rather than the rival rugby code by eight votes to five. In their early years, the team wore the claret, salmon pink and light blue jerseys of the parent club, presumably because players could readily buy these from the local gents' outfitters that supplied members of the rowing club.

BRIGHTON & HOVE ALBION 1934

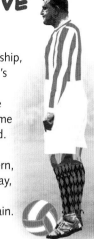

In an early example of kit sponsorship, a local business provided Brighton's kits for an FA Cup match in 1934, presumably in return for extensive advertising in the match programme and around the Goldstone Ground. The socks provided were in what appears to have been argyle pattern, popular at the time. Needless to say, these were not met with universal approval and were never seen again.

BRIGHTON & HOVE ALBION 1991–2

Brighton's traditional shirts are blue and white stripes, a fine combination that stretches back to 1904. Striped shorts are something of a rarity (for good reason) and here we see what happens when they are worn with striped shirts.

'I am glad you feature this kit because it was truly horrible, much worse than the "Chewit wrapper" away kit that normally gets a mention.'

TIM CARDER, Chairman, Brighton & Hove Albion Collectors' and Historians' Society

☞ The question is, where does shirt end and shorts begin?
Brighton & Hove Albion Collectors' and Historians' Society

BRIGHTON & HOVE ALBION AWAY 1991-2

Now that Tim mentions it, this volume would be incomplete without the infamous 'Chewit' shirt, so named because it resembled the wrapper of one of those colourful confections that were so popular at the time.

👆 Steve Gatting looks suitably embarrassed in his sweetie wrapper, not overly helped by the sponsor. © Offside

BRISTOL ROVERS 1996-7

In 1931 Bristol Rovers turned out in blue and white quartered shirts for the first time, a design intended to make the players look bigger. This style was dropped in the 1960s when it was considered old-fashioned, but made a welcome return in 1973. The problem for designers in the 1990s, who were concerned with innovation at the expense of tradition, was what to do with this iconic shirt. The good people at Cica came up with this appalling design, dubbed by supporters as the 'Tesco Bag Shirt'. It was retired after just one season.

www.oldfootballshirts.co

BURNLEY 1894–5

There is evidence to suggest that, in European cultures at least, the colour pink is associated with the feminine while blue is considered masculine. In late Victorian society, however, pink was considered a manly colour and often featured in football strips of the period. Burnley's striped shirts were one of the more vivid examples, adorned with the crest of the Prince of Wales, a privilege granted to the club after Prince Edward dropped in to Turf Moor on a visit to Burnley in 1886. The royal crest made its last appearance in the 1914 FA Cup final, when Burnley won wearing their more familiar claret and blue jerseys.

BURNLEY 1991–2

Burnley switched from their supposedly unlucky green jerseys to claret and blue in 1910 and, aside from an aberration in the late 1930s when they wore white shirts and black shorts, these have been their colours ever since. The madness that overtook kit designers in the early 1990s affected even this most conservative of clubs, who were persuaded by Ribero to adopt this horrid explosion-in-a-paint-shop interpretation of their traditional shirts.

BURTON UNITED 1904–5

Burton United were formed by a merger of the old Burton Swifts and Burton Wanderers clubs, both of which played in the Football League. United played in a variety of unusual colours including these quartered shirts in green and 'indian red', a colour usually described in these more politically correct times as chestnut brown. There is no connection with the modern Burton Albion club.

www.oldfootballshirts.com

CAMBUSLANG 1879–80

 # CAMEROON 2002

At first glance there is little that is remarkable about the strip worn by Cambuslang FC, a team based in what is now a suburb of Glasgow. They were founder members of the Scottish Football League in 1890, resigned after two seasons and were wound up in 1897. The unique feature of their otherwise unremarkable kit was the white hose registered with the Scottish FA in 1879, otherwise unheard of. In fact it was 75 years before white socks became commonplace.

In the 2002 Africa Cup of Nations, Cameroon caused a minor sensation by playing in sleeveless shirts, designed by Puma. Reaction to these innovative, figure-hugging tops was mixed: while some supporters raved about the innovative look, others compared them unfavourably to basketball tops. The final word went to FIFA spokesperson, Keith Cooper, who said, 'They are not shirts . . . they're vests.' Cameroon were required to add black sleeves for the World Cup qualifiers.

FIFA's decision upset at least one observer:

'I was really excited at seeing the sleeveless Cameroon shirts introduced just before the 2006 World Cup finals. Not only did they show off the players' wonderful, rippling biceps but also the whole "look" was really stylish and colourful. Even though I'm not a huge football fan, I was SO cross when I heard that the shirts had been banned, and thought how petty it was not to allow the sleeveless format. For this reason alone, this is my worst kit!'

ANGELA BICKERTON, football widow

☞ FIFA may not be much cop at dealing with institutional corruption or goal-line technology, but at least they will come down like a ton of bricks on silliness like this. © Offside

CAMEROON 2004

Having been chastised by FIFA for wearing sleeveless tops in 2002, one might imagine that the Cameroon Football Federation and their imaginative kit partner, Puma, would have learned their lesson.

Oh dear me no.

For the 2004 Africa Cup of Nations tournament, Puma provided a svelte one-piece shirt and shorts combo that did not go down terribly well at the guardians of world football (whose president, Sepp Blatter, let's remind ourselves, proposed that women footballers wear skimpier shorts to attract more attention around this time). When the Cameroon side wore their one-piece strips in the World Cup qualifiers, FIFA declared the outfit illegal, slapped fines on the Cameroon Football Federation and docked the team 6 points. Puma took the case to court arguing that FIFA regulations do not stipulate that shirts and shorts have to be separate, but lost. Two-piece kits were then reintroduced and FIFA rescinded the points penalty.

CARDIFF CITY AWAY 1972-3

 This mauve and yellow outfit caused gasps from Cardiff supporters when it was first seen, anticipating the trend for nasty colour combinations in away kits by 20 years. Ych y fi!

👆 Cameroon and Puma provoked FIFA even further with this one-piece effort. But how do you get it on?
© Offside

CARLISLE UNITED AWAY 1993–5

In 1993, Carlisle United adopted these famous 'deckchair shirts', which fall into the category of being so bad they are good. The following season the club won promotion and wore these shirts in the Auto Windscreens Trophy final at Wembley, so it is not surprising they are very popular with supporters and were revived in 2007.

☞ www.classicfootballshirts.co.uk

CELTIC AWAY 1991–2

By tradition, the colour palette for Celtic's change strips has generally been restricted to green and white (and since 1970, yellow). This extraordinary Umbro effort from 1991, which was worn for just one season, typifies the contemporary drive to come up with novel designs that would look good worn with jeans, but on the pitch, were crap.

☞ www.classicfootballshirts.co.uk

CELTIC AWAY 1994–5

This Umbro design incorporates the full combination of Celtic colours into a strikingly dramatic outfit that verges on the embarrassing.

☞ www.oldfootballshirts.com

CEREZO OSAKA 1998-99

The name (pronounced *Seresso Osaka*) was chosen by public competition to replace the club's original, rather less romantic moniker of Yanmar Diesel in 1993. Cerezo means cherry blossom in Japanese, so pink was the natural choice for the team to play in. This shirt was designed by Mizuno, a Japanese sportswear company that also supplied several Scottish clubs around this time. The team play in the J-League.

 www.oldfootballshirts.com

 ## CHARLTON ATHLETIC AWAY 1997-8

Charlton's choice of home kits has generally been conservative, sticking to traditional red shirts and white shorts for most of their history. In common with many clubs, Charlton experimented with radical designs for their away strips in the 1990s, including this particularly ugly design from 1997–8.

 www.oldfootballshirts.com

CHELSEA AWAY 1990-1

Chelsea have long been innovators of kit design. The combination of royal blue shirts and shorts with white socks adopted in 1964 has become the definitive Chelsea home strip. Some of the team's away strips are almost as iconic, with a couple of exceptions. This nasty red and white outfit is one.

☞ It's always tricky when the colour scheme of the ball matches that of the shirt. Just ask Clive Allen. © Offside

CHELSEA AWAY 1995-6

'Ruud Gullit, one of the all time great players signs for Chelsea. A lovely summer day. We wait in anticipation. Out he strides in his pjs! We are dumbstruck. This is a joke, yes? No, the wonderful orange and grey away kit is born. BBC Radio Five's 606 with Danny Baker has an 'open mike' to discuss this kit. One caller decided to pen a song, 'The Tangerine and Graphite'. I recently grabbed it from my collection (I have an original worn by Gullit) and I found myself almost fondling it and discovered that 15 years later I loved this polyester beast. Instantly I thought of Ruud against Newcastle in the FA Cup that season. I realised that football kits, good or bad, can transport you back in time, provoking good or bad memories. If Man United can dig out their green and gold, what price on Chelsea playing in retro tangerine and graphite in 100 years? Mmm, perhaps not.'

RICHARD BOULERT, Chelsea fan and collector

Gullit is mystified as the referee cautions the normally placid Dennis Wise for, presumably, wearing orange with grey – sorry, tangerine with graphite. © Offside

CHESTERFIELD TOWN 1892-3

Although Chesterfield Town were wound up in 1915, historians recognise this club as the precursor of the modern Chesterfield FC. These extraordinary shirts were found, according to John Taylor's research, in the loft of the Spital Hotel and may have been the property of the defunct Spital FC, whose members had been instrumental in forming the new club in 1884. Rather than throw them out, the landlord donated the shirts to the Chesterfield Town club.

CLAPTON ORIENT 1904-5

The Os have changed their name no fewer than five times since their formation as Orient FC in 1888. In 1904/05, as Clapton Orient, they were in the Second Division of the Southern League. After their first application to join the Football League was roundly rejected, a motion was passed to extend the Second Division and they were elected at the second attempt. Sadly, they dropped these unique green, red and white shirts in favour of prosaic white ones for their first season in the Football League.

CLYDEBANK 1991-2

In 1964 the owners of East Stirlingshire FC, the Steedman brothers, merged their club with Clydebank Juniors and moved lock, stock and barrel to Kilbowie Park where they played as ES Clydebank. Legal action by Shire supporters led to East Stirlingshire returning to Falkirk a year later but the Steedmans decided to remain in Clydebank and join the ranks of senior clubs. A year later Clydebank FC were elected to the long-standing vacancy in the Scottish Second Division.

During their short career, the Bankies played in some interesting kits based on their colours of red, white and black. Kilbowie Park became the first all-seater stadium in the UK after benches were installed on the terraces while the team reached the Scottish Premier League twice and discovered one of Scotland's finest players, Davie Cooper.

After the Steedmans sold the ground for development, Clydebank spent years playing home games in Dumbarton and Greenock where, due to a supporters' boycott, just 29 supporters watched their opening game at Cappielow Park. Bankrupt, homeless and on the verge of extinction,

www.oldfootballshirts.com

Clydebank were bought out by the owners of the new Airdrie United club in 2002 and replaced the now-extinct Airdrieonians in Scottish Division Two.

These shirts, worn in 1991/92 would have been a sensible all-red until the designer's 4-year-old got hold of the drawings after a bad day at playgroup.

COLCHESTER TOWN 1913

Formed in 1873, 'the Oysters' were one of many amateur teams that thrived in Essex up until the First World War, including strong Army sides from the regiments that were garrisoned in the town over the years. Colchester Town had an undistinguished history but in 1912/13, wearing these wonderful myrtle green, dark claret and white shirts, they won the South Essex League, the Essex & Suffolk Border League, the East Anglian League and the Worthington Evans Cup.

In 1936 the committee formed a professional section but Essex County FA rules would not allow a single club to operate as both amateur and professionals. Town were wound up while the pro section became Colchester United.

COVENTRY CITY 1922-4

After the First World War, Coventry hovered just above the relegation zone from Division Two season after season. In a fit of municipal enthusiasm and in an attempt to improve their fortunes, they dropped their pale blue and white colours in favour of the light green and red of the City of Coventry in March 1922. The civic coat of arms appeared on their new shirts and the entire ground was repainted in the new colours; even the new programme featured a red and green cover. Results did not improve and all that paint went to waste when they switched back to blue and white for 1924/25 and were relegated at the end of the season.

COVENTRY CITY AWAY 1975-6

In the mid-1970s, Admiral Sportswear revolutionised kit design in the UK with their innovative designs, which for the first time were branded with the manufacturer's trademark clearly visible. In fact, it was Admiral that kick-started the whole replica kit market with (not so) cheap and cheerful copies of their shirts that were soon appearing on every school playing field in the country. One of their most iconic was the 'tramline' design adopted by Coventry, Dundee and the Welsh national team to name just a few. When Coventry took to the field in this chocolate version, they were met with howls of derision (not to mention unsavoury chants) and the outfit has passed into football folklore as one of the most truly awful of all time.

Nostalgia is, of course, a wonderful thing, and this strip is now regarded with such affection that the club wore a one-off chocolate strip in the final match of 2008/09 to mark their 125th anniversary.

☞ Steve Hunt demonstrates how well Coventry's chocolate kit shows up under floodlights. © Offside

COVENTRY CITY 1981-2

In 1978 the FA and Football League dropped the rule that banned shirt sponsorship and over the next few seasons sponsors' logos started to appear (Liverpool were the first English team to wear sponsored tops in 1979/80). The BBC and ITV companies, however, refused to televise matches unless the clubs removed their sponsor's details from their shirts. Coventry thought they had found a wheeze that would get round this embargo by adopting a strip that integrated the 'T' logo of their sponsor, Talbot (manufacturers of rubbish cars) into the design. The broadcasters were not as green as they were cabbage-looking and banned Coventry from the nation's TV screens until they introduced an alternative strip just for the cameras.

☞ Brian Roberts has wearing dodgy kits down to a (wait for it) T. Boom-boom! © paphotos.com

COWDENBEATH 1882-3

The team that now styles itself with a certain sense of irony, the 'Blue Brazil' is the oldest surviving club in the ancient Kingdom of Fife. They were formed by a merger of Cowdenbeath Rangers and a colliery team, Raith Rovers (there is no connection with the modern Raith Rovers). These colourful shirts were inherited from Cowdenbeath Rangers.

CRYSTAL PALACE 2007-8

'There has been no shortage of low points in Palace's history: a 9–0 thrashing at Anfield in the late 1980s; two strolls down Administration Avenue in the late 1990s and 2010; having Roger de Courcey (not to mention Nookie Bear) as celebrity supporters to name but three. None of these can compare with the jaw-dropping horror of Palace's new kit for the 2007/08 season. The rule for stripes is WEAR PROPER STRIPES. Ignoring this, Palace's stripes did not even make it to the bottom of the shirt. They looked like a bunch of South London waiters in hallucinogenic waistcoats three sizes too small.

'Such was the derision of supporters, the stripes were changed at the end of the season to the "lucky" Palace sash of the late 1970s. From there it was but a short trip into administration, relegation battle . . . and stripes again. Will we never learn?'

PETER MOOR, Crystal Palace supporter

☞ Danny Butterfield in Palace's least popular striped outfit. Thankfully the 'moustache' deflects some attention. © Offside

DARLINGTON 1991-3

In the early 1990s the Middlesbrough-based sports goods retailer, Jack Hatfield Sports, supplied several league clubs in the region. The advantage of small clubs having a local supplier is that they are not restricted to the standard templates offered by the big, multinational companies. On the other hand, it does not guarantee good design.

 www.oldfootballshirts.com

DARWEN 1879

The epic FA Cup semi-final in February 1879 between Darwen and Old Etonians marked a turning point in the history of Association Football. The Etonian side was the epitome of the gentlemen-player teams that had dominated since the formation of the FA 16 years earlier, and which drew their members from the wealthy upper classes. Darwen, on the other hand, were one of the new breed of working-class clubs springing up in Lancashire, the Midlands and the West of Scotland, owned by hard-nosed businessmen with an eye for profit and whose mills and factories provided both players and supporters. Darwen had in their ranks Fergie Suter, now acknowledged as the first ever professional footballer, while Lord Kinnaird, then Treasurer of the FA (and its future president), played for Old Etonians.

When the 'Darreners' ran out at the Oval they were greeted with hoots of derision from the well-heeled spectators because of their motley shirts and trousers cut off at the knee in place of knickerbockers; some even wore braces. The Old Etonian players were confident of victory not least because the opposition were to a man, shorter and lighter, the result of poor diet and housing. At half time they were 5–1 up but in the closing quarter of an hour Darwen's superior fitness showed and they scored four times to equalise.

After a drawn replay, Darwen returned to London a week later for the third time thanks to a public subscription that attracted hundreds of tiny contributions from local working people. Exhausted from working full shifts and long train journeys, Darwen succumbed 6–2.

Within 4 years the new breed of clubs had completely eclipsed the gentlemen-player teams and the future direction of football as a mass spectator sport rather than a leisure activity for the wealthy was set.

DEPORTIVO WANKA 2002-3

Based in Huancayo in the Peruvian Andes, Deportivo courted controversy in 2004 when they moved their home games to Cerro de Pasco, the highest city in the world at 4,380m (13,973ft). Opponents alleged this was a cynical attempt to exploit the altitude sickness and harsh conditions that would disadvantage visitors and stave off relegation from the Peruvian First Division. They were relegated anyway and when they protested, the club was suspended from all competition. The team takes its name from the Wanka tribe who once inhabited the area.

Replica Deportivo Wanka shirts are a cult item for collectors in the UK and in 2006, thousands were sold online to the complete mystification of the club spokesman who was quoted in the *Sun* newspaper as saying, 'It is very strange. Everyone in Britain seems to think we have a funny name.'

www.classicfootballshirts.co.uk

DERBY COUNTY 1884

Derby County were formed as an offshoot of Derbyshire County Cricket Club, the brainchild of William Morley, a railway clerk whose father happened to be on the committee of the cricket club. Derbyshire were going through a lean time and the prospect of generating extra revenue by hosting football matches during the winter was too good to resist. Just one year after their formation, Derby County beat mighty Aston Villa in the FA Cup and in 1888 they became founder members of the Football League.

County's first colours were those of the parent cricket club: chocolate, amber and pale blue.

DERBY COUNTY AWAY 1987-9

Towards the end of the 1980s kit manufacturers were beginning to experiment with the potential of polyester technology and its heat-printing capabilities to produce more and more complex patterns, such as this chequerboard effect, officially described as the 'World' design by Umbro.

☞ www.oldfootballshirts.com

DERBY COUNTY AWAY 1989-92

One of Umbro's more dubious contributions to the history of football shirt design was this thick 'n' thin stripy top (rather resemblant of a bar code), which was adopted by Newcastle United. Derby ordered a set as a change strip in red and black but Robert Maxwell, who was chairman at the time, is thought to have intervened because red was the colour of County's arch rivals, Nottingham Forest. This curious silver and black version was substituted, although the red shorts and socks were retained. Not only did this make the strip look unbalanced, the shirts did not offer sufficient contrast to the white home shirts to be a useful change strip so a yellow third kit had to be ordered.

www.oldfootballshirts.com

DONCASTER ROVERS 1879

In 1879 a group of young apprentices from the LNER railway works in Doncaster organised a football game against the Yorkshire Institute for the Deaf & Dumb, wearing unusual blue jerseys with yellow cross bands and blue Tam o' Shanters with red tassels. They enjoyed themselves so much that they decided to form a club to be known as Doncaster Rovers.

DONCASTER ROVERS 1992–3

'I love this scribbly-hooped curiosity. In the summer of '92 I was party to the decision-making process for a new kit for Doncaster, after being invited by the manager to cast my eye over a few alternatives and give a "fan's view". I saw it as an opportunity to get the club recognised with this eye-catching number and though I acknowledge it was a bit "out there" and was not popular with some Doncaster fans, I think it hit the spot. I can't claim that the final decision was mine but I'd like to think that my opinion counted and in some small way I know that Doncaster ran around in this kit for two years because I liked it. Sorry about that!'

CHRISTOPHER WORRALL, Donny supporter

www.oldfootballshirts.com

 DUMBARTON 1909

Candy-striped shirts enjoyed a considerable vogue after Manchester City unveiled what was thought of at the time as a revolutionary, modern style in the FA Cup final of 1955. Dig a little deeper, however, and one discovers that there is very little that is really novel in the history of football kits. Here, for example, is a Dumbarton strip from the Edwardian era that appeared more than 45 years earlier.

DUNDEE 1953
TOUR OF SOUTH AFRICA

After a successful campaign in which they won the Scottish League Cup for the second successive season, a 17-man squad headed off to South Africa along with manager George Anderson and (naturally) the board of directors for a 2-month tour that would include three Test matches against the national side. As the Dundee players prepared for their opening game against Transvaal, Anderson produced a set of brand new shirts in his own family tartan, saying, 'These will take a trick out there.' The South African press later dubbed them 'The Tartan Troops From Tayside'.

☞ TOFFS – The Old Fashioned Football Shirt Company

DUNDEE WANDERERS 1898-9

The club was formed as Dundonian FC by the merger of Johnstone Wanderers and Strathmore in 1894. When they applied to join the Scottish Second Division, Dundee FC objected until they agreed to change their name to Dundee Wanderers. After a rotten season, they finished next to last and were not re-elected. They then joined the Northern League and in 1898 switched to this dour maroon and navy blue outfit inherited from the old Johnstone Wanderers. In 1913 the club was wound up.

DUNFERMLINE ATHLETIC 1996-7

'The Dunfermline Athletic kit of 1996–97 was truly awful. For one thing, it took away our famous stripes and replaced them with squares of black and grey (which on closer inspection turned out to be black dots). Then there was the cost – at nearly £50 it was apparently the most expensive club shirt that season. The final straw was the addition of red triangles based on the logo of the manufacturer, Le Coq Sportif. The way they looked like various road signs meant the shirt became known as "the Highway Code strip". Luckily we got out of the Le Coq deal and Avec made us a great shirt the following season.'

STUART HOLLAND, Pars supporter

 www.oldfootballshirts.com

 www.oldfootballshirts.com

 # EAST FIFE 1998-9

In 1998 East Fife quit their old home and moved into the brand new Bayview Stadium, built as part of the regeneration of the Methil docks. Pleasure at their smart new home may have been slightly reduced when supporters caught sight of the new strip the team would wear in their home games, with its eye-bothering zigzag hoops. A red and blue version was produced as a change strip.

EASTVILLE ROVERS 1895-6

Rovers played in the Bristol & District League and were based at the Star Inn on Fishponds Road, now long demolished. Formed in 1883 as the Black Arabs, they changed their name to Eastville Rovers a year later after the inner suburb where they played. They were known colloquially as the 'Purdown Poachers' because of their practice of luring the best players in the city to join them. They were certainly ambitious and in 1897 they turned professional as Bristol Eastville Rovers, becoming simply Bristol Rovers a year later. In 1895 they switched from plain white shirts to these green and buff ones.

ENGLAND THIRD KIT 1992

'After five years of producing third-choice kits that remained unused, the FA found an excuse to wear pale blue against Turkey's red and white. Flushed with their own "success" in unleashing a fairly nondescript shirt, they followed that with this grotesque monstrosity. Brushing aside 120 years of mostly plain shirts, England were suddenly obliged to wear an outfit better suited to a 7-year-old on a trip to Disneyland.

www.classicfootballshirts.co.uk

'To be fair, there was a trend at the time to weave huge versions of club crests into elaborate shadow patterns, but to stretch the Three Lions diagonally over the left side of the shirt produced an almost cartoon effect. There was even a lone lion working its way around the left thigh of the shorts to appear across the buttock. Just imagine Bobby Moore receiving the World Cup from the Queen in this. Thankfully, it was only worn twice, in Czechoslovakia and Spain.'

GLEN ISHERWOOD, www.englandfootballonline.com

ENGLAND 1996 GOALKEEPER

Lurid goalkeeping kits became fashionable in the late 1990s and David Seaman's outfit, worn during Euro '96 was one of the most outrageous. It had everything – random blocks of clashing colours, 'GLAND' written vertically up the front ('ENG' being uncomfortably tucked away where only Mrs Seaman might find it) and part of the England crest disappearing into the armpit. Known as the 'Refreshers' outfit (after the fizzy sweets) this was awfulness on a heroic scale.

☞ Seaman does his best to blend into the background. © Offside

ENGLAND AWAY 1996

'This kit was to bring to an end the FA's dalliance with pale blue change strips. Although it was described as 'indigo blue', most people remember it as being grey. Chances of a new trend of similar kits plummeted when England lost a traumatic penalty shootout to Germany in the semi-final of Euro '96.

'It was worn in just three games that year alongside a horrendous multi-coloured goalkeeping outfit in a two-pronged attack on the gullibility of the ever-increasing army of replica-buying supporters. Closer inspection reveals that it was actually a two-tone striped shirt and shorts, each tone separated by thin white stripes, and on the shorts, by red and navy blue stripes, as well. The original red numbers were quickly replaced by white numbers, which were found to stand out better against the grey, sorry, indigo blue.'

GLEN ISHERWOOD,
www.englandfootballonline.com

☞ Darren Anderton models England's 'indigo' catastrophe. © Offside

EVERTON AWAY 1992-3

'Having been brought up on a diet of white or amber/yellow away kits (save for the odd silver grey effort here and there), this radical change kit caused a bit of a stir among the Goodison faithful. Originally designed around an early home kit (the 1890/91 version) this navy blue and salmon pink striped version raised a few eyebrows. The main bone of contention was that a good number of people thought the pink was a bit too close to the dreaded red for comfort. Also, due to the production process, the club motto on the badge appeared misspelled as 'Nil Satis Nisi Optimu<u>n</u>' (rather than the correct Optimu<u>m</u>). To be honest I quite liked this kit, especially after a final day 5–2 victory over Manchester City at the old Maine Road in what was Peter Beardsley's last game for Everton.'

STEVE FLANAGAN, Everton Historian

☞ © Offside

EVERTON AWAY 1994-5

'If there was a league for the worst Everton kit of all time, this effort would have won the title by September, it was that maligned by the blue half of the city. In my mind there is only one word to describe this kit: **wrong**. For an Everton strip it was wrong on so many levels that if you looked up the definition of the word 'wrong', there would be a picture of this kit sitting beneath it. It wasn't that the kit was white (Everton have a long history of white change kits) it was the added extras on the side. In fact the pattern down each flank was described around Goodison as the tyre markings of a farm vehicle – hence the nickname of the 'Tractor Tyre' kit. If anything, this strip will serve as a reminder to kit manufacturers of today as to what can happen if you design a kit after a very long liquid lunch.'

STEVE FLANAGAN again

👉 www.oldfootballshirts.com

EVERTON AWAY 2010–11

 Like a single malt whisky, a bad kit needs to be laid down to mature for a few years so that judgement can be reached in a calm and reflective manner. A rush to judgement is always risky but in the case of Everton's latest, startling 'lightning pink' shirts, launched with the usual ludicrous media hype, the risk seems worth taking. Of course, the club turned out in tasteful shades of pink in the Victorian era, but this modern interpretation will have the founders of this fine club rotating in their graves.

☞ Yakubu looking pretty in pink. 'Changing room is that-a-way boys!'
© Offside

FALKIRK 1996-7

'This chequerboard shirt was massively hated by supporters and also reflected the darkest chapter in the club's history. The chairman left amid allegations of embezzlement, leaving the club in such considerable debt that it was placed into provisional liquidation. Thanks to the efforts of a supporters' group, "Back the Bairns", Falkirk survived and with a new regime in charge, the despised strip was dropped and the crowds returned to Brockville.'

WILLIAM MOHIEDDEEN, Falkirk supporter

Falkirk reached the Scottish FA Cup final that season where they lost narrowly to Kilmarnock. They wore their traditional navy shirts and white shorts in that game.

☞ www.classicfootballshirts.co.uk

ACF FIORENTINA AWAY 1992-3

La Viola have played in their distinctive purple and white colours since 1928. Legend has it that their old red and white shirts ran after being washed in the river, giving rise to their striking colour scheme. Normally Fiorentina wear predominantly white when they have to change but in this example, the colours of their favoured home and away strips were combined along with a bizarre abstract pattern to achieve . . . well, it's hard to describe exactly what this achieved, really.

👆 Even the mighty Batistuta struggles to pull this ensemble off. © Offside

FOREST c. 1860

Formed in 1859, just two years after the world's oldest football club, Sheffield FC, Forest were pioneers. Based in and around London, they drew their players from the public schools of the era. In 1864 they fetched up in Battersea Park and became the Wanderers, one of the greatest of all the Victorian teams of gentlemen-players. The similarity of these early shirts to those worn at Harrow School is unlikely to be a coincidence. Several Forest players would have attended Harrow and likely wore their distinctive house shirts (each house at Harrow had different colours in the traditional narrow striped pattern).

FORFAR ATHLETIC 1992–4

The 1990s vogue for unsightly shirts included this geometrical design by Matchwinner that combined the Loons' traditional two shades of blue into a somewhat disturbing pattern.

👉 www.oldfootballshirts.com

GERMANY 1994

The German team has been kitted out by Adidas since 1954, whose current contract runs until 2018, a world record for longevity. An offer in 2007 by US-based Nike to outfit the team for a figure of €500m, believed to be six times what Adidas pay, was turned down by the patriotically-minded Deutscher Fußball-Bund. Adidas have generally provided elegant designs for the national team but in 1994 they were infected with the fashion for extravagance. This shirt was worn in the World Cup finals held in the USA.

👉 Markus Babbel looks a tad alarmed by Adidas' interpretation of the German flag. © Offside

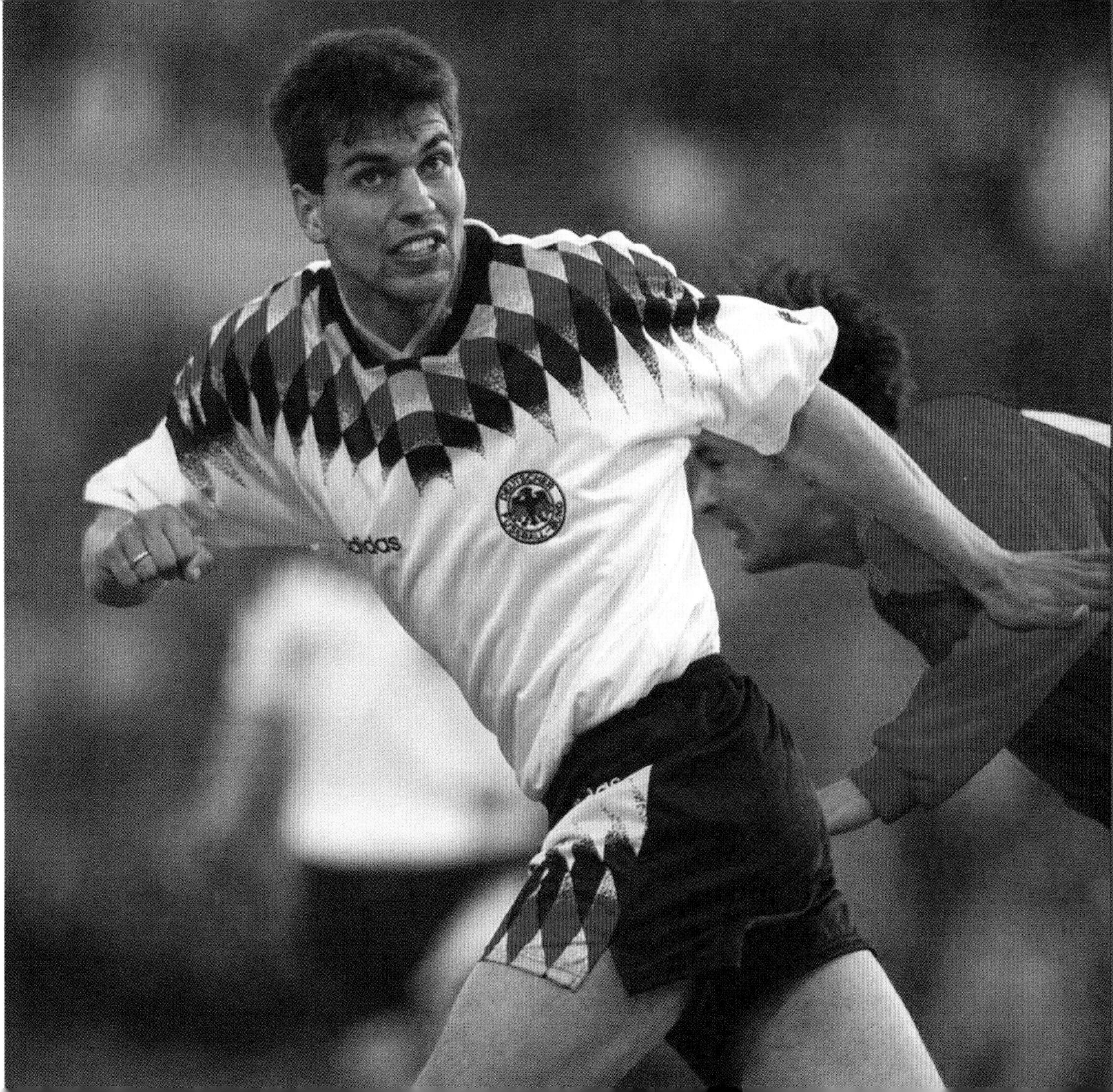

GETAFE CF SAD 2009-10

The town of Getafe forms part of the Madrid metropolitan area. The eponymous football team rose from the lowest level of the Spanish pyramid over the course of 20 years, winning promotion to La Liga in 2004 where, against all expectation, they have consolidated. Indeed, playing the elite seems to bring out the best in the team and at the time of writing they have met Real Madrid six times, winning three and losing three. Now I have nothing against the sponsor, nor their fine chain of restaurants, but there is something a little incongruous, in the current climate of concern over obesity and heart disease, about a fast food chain associating itself with a sport that requires supreme fitness levels.

Flame-grilled and extra cheesy Spanish topping? © Offside

GLENTORAN AWAY 1996-97

The 'Big Chicken Shirt' traded on the happy coincidence of the cockerel being the emblem of both the football club and the French kit manufacturer that designed it, Le Coq Sportif. It was worn when the Glens were hammered 8–0 by Sparta Prague in the European Cup Winners' Cup and was retired after a single season. Naturally it is now a cult item at the Oval.

Glentoran's big chicken. www.oldfootballshirts.com

GLOSSOP 1910-11 GREENOCK MORTON 1993-5

These days trends in football fashion come and go with astonishing rapidity but we do not associate the staid world of the Edwardians with such trivial matters. However, when Manchester United wore a smart all-white strip with a bold red chevron on their shirts in the 1909 FA Cup final, a chord was struck and the style was widely copied. The mighty Glossop FC were one of the first to jump on the bandwagon and remain the only Football League club to have featured purple as part of their first choice strip.

Although tartan had featured in the colours of some Scottish army teams in the 1870s it took 120 years before manufacturers were able to exploit the new sublimation process to mass produce tartan shirts. The national side adopted a tartan kit specially designed for the Scottish FA from 1994. Modest Greenock Morton, however, were the first Scottish team to sport tartan shirts on a regular basis. The design was revived as a third kit in 2007/08 and proved a popular seller.

www.oldfootballshirts.com

 ## HACKNEY BLACK ROVERS 1870

Practically nothing is known about this very early football team who probably played, well, in Hackney really. However, we do know they sported these wonderful, piratical tops.

HAMILTON ACADEMICALS 1908–13

It was not unusual for teams in the early part of the twentieth century to adopt the colours of aristocratic patrons. Chelsea, for example, started out in the lightish blue racing colours of the Earl of Cadogan while St Bernard's FC (who won the Scottish FA Cup in 1895) wore the primrose and pink of the Earl of Rosebery for a few years (as did the national Scottish team). The Academicals adopted the cerise and french grey racing colours of the Duke of Hamilton for four seasons before returning to their usual red and white strip.

HARROW SCHOOL 1870

The unique rules of Harrow football, which is played to this day with a curious, hassock-shaped ball, were specifically developed to accommodate the school's muddy clay pitches in the mid-eighteenth century and were a precursor to the association rules written in 1863. The annual inter-house competition was (and is still) played each spring, when the pitches have reached just the right sticky consistency. According to E.D. Laborde's *Harrow School Yesterday and Today*, 'the school football XI wore a shirt, cap and knickerbockers all with equal width black and magenta vertical stripes.' Since nobody else played by Harrow Rules, this extraordinary outfit was almost certainly worn in the annual match against a Harrow Old Boys XI.

The sons of aristocracy adopt typically languid and bored poses in 1870.

HARTLEPOOL UNITED 1991-3

This is without question one of the busiest shirts ever produced. No matter how closely you examine it, there is always something new to discover. It is basically a chequered pattern. With stripes. And it's halved and there's a big horizontal band on the chest. Did I mention the pinstripes? Or the fine sublimated stripes? And there's a butterfly . . . Nurse?

HEART OF MIDLOTHIAN 1876-7

Formed in 1873, Hearts are one of Scotland's oldest clubs. Named after a popular dance hall they originally wore white with maroon trimmings sewn into their shirts and knickerbockers. In 1876 they adopted these white, navy and red hooped jerseys with the letters MFBC (Midlothian Foot Ball Club) embroidered onto a white patch worn on the chest. These proved unpopular with the players (who had to provide their own kit), presumably because they were more expensive than the plain jerseys available from gents' outfitters at the time. The following season the embroidered patches were removed and the shirts dyed maroon: photographs show the old hoops clearly showing through.

HEREFORD UNITED AWAY 1993-4

The Bulls normally wear sober outfits of white and black when at home, occasionally with red as an accent colour. In 1993 they adopted Matchwinner's interference pattern shirt (see Reading 1991-2 entry), which was bad enough but their away kit defied belief. Chosen by the club chairman, it was meant to steal a march on rivals Shrewsbury's extravagant yellow and blue shirt and was worn when Hereford were knocked out of the FA Cup by non-league Bath City. Not a top remembered with much affection at Edgar Road then.

HIBERNIAN AWAY 1977–8

'Hibs' purple Bukta change strips of the late 1970s were not without their fans. Purple, after all, was a quintessential '70s colour along with bottle green, orange and brown. Think Gilbert O'Sullivan, *Abigail's Party*, those old bedroom curtains. For most, however, the strip took garish over-embellishment and colour mixing to an unacceptable extreme. It shared the same design philosophy as Admiral tops of the era, looking too easily wearable by DLT presenting *Top of the Pops*. Coinciding as it did with the emergence of the punk style revolution, it was sartorially stillborn, reeking of medallion-man and impossible to wear without matching Noddy Holder sideburns, shoulder-length mane and big bushy 'tache. Most of the Hibs players in 1978 still fitted that description but they were a team in decline, adding negative association to the evident aesthetic handicap. The final nail was the abrasive nylon fabric, which practically invented nipple-rash and exposed the wearer to serious risk of self-electrocution.'

FRASER PETTIGREW,
Hibs exile in
New Zealand

HIBERNIAN 1994–5

'Despite being contrived only in the late 1930s, Hibernian's white sleeves have become an untouchable feature of the club's visual identity for fans. As if the defilement of the sacred sleeves was not enough in this 1994 variation, the execution renders a beautifully simple strip in terms redolent of a barbershop quartet or a fast food franchise uniform. Not content with its primary abomination, the design failure is compounded in a Frankensteinian assembly of disparate parts: a non-complementary strip of Mitre chevrons runs around the cuff and an entirely different zigzag strip through the collar. Chevrons around the hem of the shorts impart a frilly-knicker effect. The plastic popper-button neck vainly attempts to appropriate some retro-classic collar style but it's as futile and incongruous as grafting an imitation Rolls-Royce grille onto an Austin Princess. The best anyone could say about it is that it's better than any Hearts strip ever made.'

FRASER PETTIGREW again

 Fraser Pettigrew www.classicfootballshirts.co.uk

HUDDERSFIELD TOWN AWAY 1991-2

 The Terriers are a club with considerable pedigree, having won the FA Cup in 1922 followed by an unprecedented hat-trick of league championships in 1924, 1925 and 1926 under Herbert Chapman, one of the greatest managers of all time. After the Second World War the club fell on hard times but they remain ambitious and were among the first English clubs to build a brand new stadium. Since the 1960s the team's favoured change strip has been red and black, of which this example, with electric hoops is certainly the most striking.

 # HULL CITY 1992-3

'For a kit to permeate the national psyche usually requires a team to perform laudable exploits while wearing it; win a major trophy, secure promotion, or at least embark upon a plucky cup run. Not so with Hull City's 1992–3 strip, worn during two seasons of unspectacular, lower-league mediocrity. It was purely the design that secured this kit's enduring infamy, as Scottish brand Matchwinner looked to the club's nickname for inspiration and produced a lurid tiger stripe print shirt. Though universally mocked, this shirt is much loved by Tiger Nationals, who revel in the kitsch value and remember the media tumult generated as a rare bright spot in an otherwise bleak decade.

'Oft forgotten is the club's ill-advised attempt to replicate the design following an acrimonious split and legal wrangle with Matchwinner. Successors Pelada "reinterpreted" this commercially successful shirt and somehow produced a rusty brown, leopard spotted abomination that is truly our worst kit, though it's the 1992 shirt that gets the pop-culture profile.'

LES MOTHERBY,
www.ambernectar.org

www.oldfootballshirts.com

1990s kitsch at its very best.
www.ambernectar.org

JUVENTUS AWAY 1997–8

Juve originally played in pink shirts and black knickers when they were formed in 1897. In 1903, after their original tops became too faded to wear, one of their members, Englishman John Savage, contacted a friend in Nottingham who in turn had contacts at Notts County, and he arranged for a set of black and white striped tops to be shipped to Italy. These have remained the colours of *La Vecchia Signora* (The Old Lady) to this day but in 1997, to mark their centenary, a replica of the original shirts was introduced as a change kit, with an accurate recreation of the original collar alongside modern fripperies such as a club crest and shirt sponsorship. I must admit, this is actually not a bad kit, just rather unexpected.

☞ Alessandro Del Piero dressed as a pink Old Lady. © Offside

1. FC KAISERSLAUTERN 1993–4

It was not just in the UK that poorly designed kits became the norm during the 1990s. Indeed, it can be argued that the German Bundesliga led the world in ugly kits as well as producing world-beating players during the decade. This example shows how a good basic design concept can be ruined by over-elaborate detailing

☞ Jan Eriksson's shirt combines almost every feature it is possible to imagine including, it would appear, a smiley mouth. © Offside

THE WORST FOOTBALL KITS OF ALL TIME

 # LEEDS CITY 1910-11

On the face of it there is nothing remarkable about this outfit of plain green jerseys and white knickers. It is the story behind it that justifies a place in the pantheon of bad kits. City's colours had been navy blue and old gold since their formation in 1904. On 5 September 1910 the *Leeds Mercury* reported that five young and inexperienced players had been signed for the first team from Irish clubs Cliftonville, Distillery (based in Ulster) and Shelbourne (from Dublin). The report went on to say, 'Mr Scott-Walford [the club's secretary/manager] evidently had an eye to making his new men feel at home . . . when he attired the team in green jerseys and supplied green flags to mark the centreline.' What is not recorded is how this gesture went down with the players. Since Association Football was largely played in Ulster at the time (regarded as the 'garrison game' in the south where Gaelic Football and Hurling were preferred) and the Irish national team played in blue, it cannot be assumed that these gestures were welcome.

LEEDS UNITED AWAY 1994-5

'In 1993 United introduced a new-look blue and gold hoop to their jerseys and in keeping with this theme, the away shirt bore blue and gold stripes. The change strip resulted in a number of colour clashes so it was swapped in 1994 for distinctive navy and green stripes. This outfit was dumped unceremoniously after a cup-tie at Bolton when the players complained the colours were too dark and made it difficult to pick each other out. On the other hand Leeds fans won't hear a word against the navy and green, claiming it as a "cracking kit" worn during some of the team's best performances, including Tony Yeboah's hat-trick in a UEFA cup match in Monaco.'

DAVE TOMLINSON,
www.mightyleeds.co.uk

Tony Yeboah shows off Leeds' invisible outfit.
© Offside

LEYTON ORIENT 1998-9

Portuguese side Boavista FC have worn chequered shirts in black and white for many years but this design has, perhaps understandably, failed to catch on elsewhere. One or two senior teams in the UK have at some stage experimented with chequered patterns for their away strips but Leyton Orient are the only English club to have worn this style as a home strip. The Os have a long tradition of wearing unconventional outfits and this was probably the most outrageous, appearing for the first time in 1998. It must have pleased many home supporters because in 2001 it was revived under the club's own brand name.

www.oldfootballshirts.com

LI JIANG (v GUILIN) 1988

'In 1988 I was happily cycling through the Chinese countryside with my wife and we were beginning to enjoy our strange surroundings. Somehow we had managed to negotiate our way through the city and the flow of thousands of other cyclists who seemed miraculously to divide like the Red Sea as we approached. I had also become accustomed to the 360° swivel of my bicycle seat – after nearly falling off into a paddy field and many bemused water buffalo – and felt a million miles away from the hurly-burly of the English football season.

'Then, after climbing a small hill, there in front of us was a huge sports stadium. I sped up a little and persuaded my long-suffering wife to check out the interior – and yes, there was even a match in progress.

'I must make it clear at this moment, I have an all-engaging hobby of collecting club colours (since the early 1950s) and seeing two new strips filled me with great excitement. Unfortunately, that's when the problems started. Firstly, despite the obvious importance and quality of the game, there were only about half a dozen spectators. I wanted to know the names of the two teams but there was no public information, my new companions didn't speak a word of English and my limited grasp of Chinese consisting of "good day" and "how are you?" weren't going to get me very far.

'However, I did know from experience that smaller Chinese teams usually wore the club name across the chests of their shirts, but of course, these were in Chinese characters. Undaunted, I spent the next hour trying to write down this script accurately on a piece of paper, continually making corrections to minute details. And despite the fact that Chinese players never seem to stop moving, eventually I had all the strokes and shapes onto my paper.

'I rushed back to the other spectators who, happily, were as excited as I was about this new cultural interchange and I was rewarded with "Li Jiang" (plus the word for 'Region') and "Guilin" (plus the word for 'City' and confirmed which was the team in red and which wore white shirts.

'The kits themselves, in all fairness, were not the worst I've ever seen but the process of discovery had certainly been one of the worst in terms of traumatic endeavour. We never found out why there were only eight of us there, or even the score, but as I clutched my piece of paper on the way back, I hoped I would never have to put so much effort into adding two more strips to my collection of thousands!'

BOB BICKERTON

Bob Bickerton

LINCOLN CITY 1885

Lincoln City emerged in 1884 following the collapse of Lincoln Rovers who, along with Lindum FC, were one of the leading teams in the city at the time. The new club inherited the red and white striped shirts of the Rovers club as well as several of their players. At the time players provided their own kit and, in what may have been an attempt to assert their individuality, they sometimes customised their kit. Either that or there were problems getting consistent designs from their suppliers. A photograph of the team from 1885 shows the majority wearing conventional narrow stripes of the period but several players are wearing these bewildering combinations of vertical and horizontal stripes.

LINCOLN CITY 2001-2

'The shorts for this kit were originally red when unveiled at the end of the previous season. This proved very unpopular as the club had asked for votes and the response was overwhelmingly in favour of black. As editor of the club fanzine, I led the protest and was invited to meet the chairman. He asked me to cool the criticism (the shirt was nothing like what the fans had voted for either) and in return the club would go with black shorts. The kit was supposed to be changed after two years but was so unpopular they kept the not much better away shirt and changed the home one. Since then they have been much more faithful to the wishes of fans for red and white stripes, black shorts and red socks.'

JAMES BRIDE, editor of *The Deranged Ferret* fanzine

 www.oldfootballshirts.com

LIVERPOOL 1892-6

Whisper it softly on Merseyside but it is true: Liverpool started out wearing blue and white. Not only that, but the strips had previously belonged to Everton and had been left behind when they quit Anfield after a row about the rent. John Houlding, a local brewer and owner of the stadium, formed Liverpool FC to fill the gap and must have been delighted to find the abandoned shirts in the changing rooms, which meant he would not have to go to the expense of buying new kit for his team. It was not until 1896 that Liverpool adopted the municipal red that they made famous. Another reason for the choice of colours was that at this time Everton were wearing red shirts. Oh the irony!

LIVERPOOL 1991-2

In 1991 Adidas attempted to reinvent itself with a more 'modern' image. The famous trefoil trademark was replaced with a new 'Adidas Equipment' logo and the iconic three-stripe trim was dropped in favour of far bolder designs. Typical of these was this strip worn by Liverpool with three bold diagonal stripes on shirt and shorts. Many of the Anfield faithful disliked this strip (and the version that followed it two seasons later) because the hefty three-stripe motif completely dominated the kit at the expense of their team's traditional appearance. Within a few seasons, Adidas appeared to rethink this radical approach and reintroduced the popular striped trim on shoulders and sleeves.

Liverpool's emblem, the sponsor and Mark Walters all seem to be in the way of the rather prominent Adidas three stripes – how rude!
© Offside

FC LORIENT
THIRD KIT 2009-10

Football Club Lorient Bretagne Sud, to give them their proper title, play in the top tier of the French Football League and make much of their status as representatives of Brittany on the national stage. Their normal colours are dark orange and black with a white change strip. Just in case there is a clash (unlikely I know) a third strip was introduced for the 2009/10 season in chocolate and light blue. The fishing net motif no doubt evokes Brittany's association with seafood (and excellent it is but only in France would gastronomy contribute to kit design), while the entire ensemble is disfigured with excessive advertising. Note also the extraordinary cut of the waistline, which makes replicas impossible to wear by all but mermaids.

www.oldfootballshirts.com

LUTON TOWN
1899-1901

We associate pinstriped shirts with the 1980s but studies of the history of football kits reveal that the Victorians pioneered many styles that are now considered modern. Here, for example, is the Luton strip worn at the turn of the twentieth century.

LUTON TOWN 1991-2

'I bought one of these for my son's fourth birthday in 1992 (discounted, of course) and have always blamed the shirt for his lack of interest in Luton. The embarrassment of being forced to wear it must have been acute at that age. In fact the blue and orange daubs on the front always reminded me of his painting smock at play school. While it is quite restrained in comparison to some contemporary kits it is comfortably Luton's least appealing strip.'

SIMON MONKS, Luton Town supporter and historian

☞ Luton's shell-suit tribute. © Offside

MACKENZIE 1867

Contrary to popular belief, the FA Cup is not the world's oldest football competition: this distinction goes to the Youdan Cup, contested in Sheffield in 1867 under the Sheffield Rules. These differed from the FA Rules in several ways, not least by having a goal just 4 yards wide with a second set of posts 2 yards further along the goal line on each side. If the ball passed between the inner and outer posts a 'rouge' was scored, which counted only if the teams were level on goals scored.

Mackenzie were one of twelve teams to compete for the trophy, which was donated by Thomas Youdan, a theatre manager. The trophy was believed lost until it turned up in the hands of a Scottish antiques collector in 1997, who sold it to the original winners, Hallam FC, for £2,000.

MANCHESTER CITY AWAY 1996-7

Since the mid-1980s, City have worn some startling away strips of which this eyebrow-raiser is but a sample. Featuring no fewer than five colours it was worn when City were struggling in the second tier and Steve Coppell resigned after just six matches in charge.

☞ www.classicfootballshirts.co.uk

MANCHESTER CITY AWAY 1998-9

City's troubles on and off the pitch in the 1990s took them down to Division Two (the third tier), at the end of the 1997/98 season. At the time their kit supplier was Kappa, who produced a vivid 'lazer blue' home shirt and this outrageous fluorescent yellow and navy away shirt with light blue detailing. By any standards this combination of colours was appalling and ought to have been subject to the some sort of warning before being broadcast on TV. City fans are unlikely to share this view since their team wore it at Wembley in the play-off final against Gillingham when they came back from two goals down to win on penalties and start the long journey back to the Premier League.

☞ www.classicfootballshirts.co.uk

MANCHESTER UNITED AWAY 1995-6

'The kit that defied the odds! The initial concept was flawed – to maximise replica kit sales the design should compliment denim jeans. Few, if any, grey kits had worked before Umbro's designers combined at least three shades of grey, added a pin stripe to the shirt and shorts, and of course the essential collar for Cantona. Yet somehow it worked, not as an all-time classic but certainly not as one of the worst kits either. True it looked horrendous when combined with the white shorts and socks, as at the Dell, and therein lays its infamy. Conceding three first half goals at Southampton during a tense title run-in demands an explanation and obviously the kit was to blame – if the players couldn't see each other how could they pick out a pass? United never wore the kit again. One of the worst kits of all time? No, but it would make the top three of any list of worst excuses for a defeat.'

PAUL NAGEL, www.unitedkits.com

☞ United's grey shirts, teamed with their white home shorts, prompted Sir Alex Ferguson's fury after a dismal performance at Southampon and was never seen again. © Offside

THE WORST FOOTBALL KITS OF ALL TIME

 ## MANCHESTER UNITED 1996-7

'Only the third home kit produced by Umbro but it appears their design team had already run out of ideas, although the replacement of the double diamond trademark by the word Umbro suggested that this was a kit they were especially proud of. Even with the passage of time I struggle to find a single redeeming feature. The overall impression is a simplistic, almost childish design, with broad bold stripes on the shorts and thick bands on the socks. The black smudges on the shirt sides and sleeves suggest the frequent use of a poor quality eraser as the designer struggled to "perfect" the shirt. Somehow the smudges made it through to the finished kit! Facing a second season in this monstrosity, Cantona chose the honourable course and retired. Sadly the Umbro design team learned few lessons from this disaster and managed to go one worse in their fourth, and final, design.'

PAUL NAGEL, www.unitedkits.com

☞ The kit that saw off Cantona? Gary Neville doesn't seem to mind it, though. © Offside

 ## MANCHESTER UNITED 2009-10

Nike launched this controversial shirt on the back of United having played at Old Trafford for 100 years and stated that it was modelled on the shirts worn at the time. When the author, among others, challenged the club to provide some evidence of this (United's past kits have been researched in considerable detail by local historians) there was a deafening silence but the text on the club's website changed overnight. The chevron, it transpires, was not 'modelled on' but 'inspired by' the kit worn in the 1909 FA Cup final, which was in fact white with a red V. In marketing circles the term 'inspired by' can be used to imply just about anything.

☞ Wayne Rooney demonstrates his versatility by biting his nails and fondling his groin while wearing United's dubious chevron shirt. © Offside

 # MEXICO – JORGE CAMPOS' GOALKEEPER KIT 1994

Jorge Francisco Campos Navarrete, to give him his full name, achieved legendary status in his native Mexico for his acrobatic, if not eccentric approach to goalkeeping. At just 1.68m (5ft 6in) he was possibly the smallest goalkeeper to achieve international success. He frequently played well out of his goal and at club level would often switch midway through a game from goalkeeper to striker. 'Chiqui-Campos' came to world attention when he played for the Mexican national side wearing one of his trademark kits, which he designed himself. When Campos finally retired from international football in 2004 with 130 caps, everyone on the substitutes' bench wore one of his typically garish strips in his honour.

☞ The great and inimitable Campos in one of his typically understated goalkeeper outfits.
© Offside

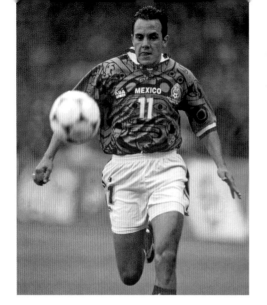

 ## MEXICO 1998

When Mexico played in the 1998 World Cup finals, they wore their traditional colours of green shirts, white shorts and red socks with one significant addition. The shirts were emblazoned with a jacquard print representing the Aztec Sunstone (also known as the Calendar Stone) which was excavated from the centre of Mexico City in 1790. Wearing a national treasure on your shirts seems a bit tacky. After all, you wouldn't expect to see England wearing big cartoon lions or the cross of St George printed into their shirts. What's that? They did? Oh dear.

☞ © Offside

 ## MIDDLESBROUGH 1889

As professionalism swept through the north in the late 1880s, the committee of Middlesbrough FC remained staunchly faithful to their amateur principles, leading dissenting members to form a breakaway club, Middlesbrough Ironopolis, in 1889. Rivalry between the two was bitter and after a proposal from the professional club to merge the two teams was rejected, Middlesbrough themselves briefly turned professional in an attempt to drive their rivals out of business. Fortune seemed to favour the Ironopolis team who were elected to the Football League in 1893 but they resigned at the end of the season and went out of business, leaving Middlesbrough FC as the dominant force in the town. This outfit, with dainty polka dots on the collar, was worn at the time of the split.

MIDDLESBROUGH IRONOPOLIS 1889

The professional offspring of Middlesbrough FC took to the field in their first season wearing these unusual maroon and green shirts. Their splendid name, redolent of the town's reputation as a centre for steelmaking, gave rise to their nickname of 'The Nops'. This also happens to mean 'washers' (i.e. small coins) in local dialect, a more than suitable soubriquet for the players who had, in the view of the older club, sold out their principles to play for money.

MIDDLESBROUGH AWAY 1996-7

Like so many clubs with strong traditions attached to their home strips (when polled, Boro's fans invariably vote in favour of wearing red shirts with the white chest band that Jack Charlton introduced in 1973), Middlesbrough make a point of being more experimental with their away kits. This Errea design featured a bold, off-centre cross with an elaborate abstract pattern. 'Boro' was picked out as a pale shadow print on the shorts, echoing the design of the version worn with the home strip.

Ian might be Wright, but I think Robbo would say this kit is just wrong. © Offside

AS MONACO 2007-8

In September 2006 Norbert Teufelberger and Manfred Bodner, the founders of Bwin, the online betting company, were on their way to a press conference to launch their sponsorship of AS Monaco, but instead of greeting the awaiting press, they found themselves thrown into a French gaol.

The authorities, particularly the French betting monopoly, PMU, were furious that internet gambling groups like Bwin were evading French gaming laws and were determined to crack down. Within weeks French football's governing body had banned sponsorship by online casinos, forcing Nantes and Toulouse to remove their sponsors' logos from their shirts (Toulouse replaced 888.com with '???.com-CENSORED' – the authorities were not amused). Teufelberger and Bodner were released on bail

www.oldfootballshirts.com
(embellished by author)

a few days later but they faced up to 3 years in prison if found guilty of breaching French gaming laws. Meanwhile the row has escalated into a confrontation between the big online casinos, backed by EU law and national member states determined to enforce national regulation. And this is a mock up of the shirt that never was, which started it all off.

NETHERLANDS 1988

Despite the enormous talent that has been available in the Dutch side since the 1970s, the European Championship of 1988 is the only international competition they have won to date. The team play in orange (the colour of the royal house), which usually looks rather smart, although being confronted by massed ranks of Dutch supporters all wearing bright orange gear can be disconcerting

(after encountering half-a-dozen orange Smurfs at Schiphol airport one afternoon, I had to be helped onto my flight). The shirts worn in the 1988 tournament featured a typical, unsightly geometric pattern of the period.

'Clap and smile boys, celebrate your achievement, enjoy the moment – just don't look down.' © Offside

NEWCASTLE UNITED AWAY 1997-8

To change the mighty Toon's traditional black and white home strip is unthinkable, but in the 1990s all sorts of interesting away kits were introduced, including the memorable dark red and navy hooped retro shirts inspired by the kit worn by Newcastle West End, one of the club's antecedents, in 1995. This outfit, however, stretched the boundaries a little too far.

☞ Ian must have been in a Rush (geddit?) to change out of this kit. © Offside

NEWCASTLE UNITED AWAY 2009-10

After a season of total management chaos, Newcastle were relegated from the Premier League in 2009 and chairman Mike Ashley became Tyneside's least popular citizen (try saying *persona non grata* in a broad Geordie accent to get the full effect). To add insult to injury, the club introduced this ludicrous banana and custard away kit for their Championship campaign. Normally Toon fans queue all night to get their hands on each season's new strip but thanks to a boycott, just three supporters presented themselves on launch day and within a week replicas were being discounted by 20 per cent in the club store.

☞ Nothing yellow here, it takes real courage to pull off the custard cream look. © Offside

NEWPORT COUNTY SEPTEMBER 1938

The Ironsides generally wore the municipal colours of amber and black during their career, colours shared with the rather more successful local rugby union team, with whom they waged a long and ultimately futile battle for support. After losing their Football League place in 1931 they were elected back into Division Three (South) in 1932 but were forced to seek re-election three times in the next four seasons. A change of colours (to red and white) in 1935 did nothing to improve their fortunes and in 1938 the board decided to revert to their traditional colours but in a novel design of amber shirt with three black bands. It appears there was an unfortunate misunderstanding with their kit supplier because when the new shirts arrived, the colours were reversed. County played in these tops until the correct shirts were delivered a month later. This did the trick and Newport finished the season as champions.

NEWTON STEWART ATHLETIC 1891–5

Based in Newton Stewart, Wigtownshire, Athletic were formed in 1881 and disappeared 21 years later, having made little impression. Their chocolate and grey shirts do, however, deserve to be remembered.

NIKE GOALKEEPER KIT (WORLD CUP 2010)

Ever since Spurs ran out for the 1991 FA Cup wearing long shorts, the hems on these important items of kit have steadily got lower. Currently they are generally worn just above the knee, a stark contrast to the

skimpy versions fashionable in the 1960s, '70s and '80s. During the 2010 World Cup, a new landmark was achieved by teams sponsored by Nike, who supplied kits to the goalkeepers with generously cut 'shorts' that reached well below the knee, a style that has been absent from the game since the rules that required English players to cover their knees were dropped in 1907. To be really 'street', the socks are worn rolled up to mid-thigh as shown here by Brazilian 'keeper, Júlio César.

👉 Júlio César sports Nike's last word in big shorts – and I mean big! They're massive! Huge! Gargantuan! Do they have their own postcode? © Offside

NORTHERN IRELAND 1990-2

NORWICH CITY 1992-4

'The early 1990s was a dark time for Northern Ireland fans. The shine of the team's exploits in the 1980s had long-since worn off and attendances were plummeting. On the player front it shouldn't have been that bad; we could field a team of English First Division regulars in almost every position, but still goals scored were few and far between and at the other end were conceded with monotonous regularity.

The final straw to all this was the abomination in which the players took the field, a shirt that wouldn't have looked out of place as a table cloth beneath a 1970s fondue set. Stripes and triangles in a mint green kaleidoscopic combination proved a harsh change from the previous decade's rather staid Adidas offerings – even the badge was the wrong shade of yellow!

In the cold light of day two decades on, this shirt actually holds a place in the hearts of many of the Green and White Army and some pristine examples can still be easily picked out in the stands of Windsor Park. It could now be said that the shirt is looked back on with much more affection than the football, which reached its nadir with a 1–1 home draw with the Faroe Islands.'

JONNY DEWART, editor, www.nifootball.blogspot.com

Nigel Worthington somehow manages to look dignified, even in this shirt.
© Offside

Mark Robins looks like he may ha[ve] spent too much time in the aviary.
© Offside

'When you support a club like Norwich City, you wait a lifetime to see them reach the top, and then pray, silently inside your head, that they won't make fools of themselves. My Canaries of the early 1990s certainly didn't do that, at least not with their performances on the field. As founder members of the Premier League in the 1992/93 season they conquered, one by one, week by week, the likes of Arsenal, Everton, Chelsea, Liverpool and Aston Villa. A year later, Bayern Munich could not live with them. If only we supporters had noticed the kit they were playing in. The Ribero-produced shirt was by far the worst in our long history, and arguably the most horrific and disturbing specimen ever witnessed on an English football field. Honestly, we didn't realise. We were too busy living the dream. Only years later, when viewing the countless images of those exciting times did we spot the 'bird poo'. By then it was too late. It doesn't matter now of course, and we wouldn't swap the memories for anything. Whatever derision the shirt may have brought after the event, nobody can deny it was unique – as were the players wearing it.'

ANDREW HARRISON,
www.canaryseventyninety.blogspot.com

NORWICH CITY AWAY 1994–5

'There really was to be no escape from the gaudy imagination of the Ribero studio for this generation of Norwich City players. This design was the change shirt for the 1994 season, the chosen alternative to the iconic 'bird poo' classic (which was, incidentally, also more politely known as 'the egg and cress' or 'the pebble dash' shirt – the bird droppings reference was a scurrilous nickname for

www.oldfootballshirts.com

it, adopted by rival fans). The intentions in letting this creation escape from the aviary were honourable no doubt. Blue is a sensible back-up to yellow. It was just a shame that the end product more resembled a table cloth from a sea front café in Cromer than a shirt to be adorned by one of the best teams in the land. Thankfully, due to our first choice colours rarely clashing with other sides, it was not often seen. Sometimes it is jokingly said that the success of the Norwich team in the mid-1990s was entirely down to the shock value of their shirts, that the bright and gaudy patterns put opponents out of their stride. Not true of course, but a nice conspiracy theory nonetheless.'

ANDREW HARRISON again

NOTTS COUNTY 1950-1

On the face of it there is nothing remarkable about County's outfit from 1950. Footballers are, however, a superstitious lot and after a string of poor results at the beginning of the season, they decided to remove the brand new magpie crest from their shirts. A stylised version reappeared in 1977 but it was not until 1986 that a pair of the much-maligned creatures were incorporated into the club crest. Altogether now, 'One for sorrow, two for joy . . .'

The amber sock turnovers were, incidentally, a nod towards County's original colours and became a regular accent colour on the team's strips from 1989.

NOTTS COUNTY 1993-4

In the search for a novel variation on the black and white striped theme, Matchwinner came up with this extraordinary barcode design for the Magpies. The shirts were sponsored by Home Bitter for home games, McEwan's Lager away.

👉 www.classicfootballshirts.co.uk

OLD ETONIANS 1882

One of the outstanding gentleman-player teams of the Victorian period, Old Etonians appeared in six FA Cup finals, winning the competition twice. Their colours were Eton blue and white and for the 1882 final against Blackburn, they wore new 'harlequin' (i.e. quartered) shirts.

Their most famous player was Arthur, 11th Lord Kinnaird (right), co-founder of the Football Association and the outstanding player of the period. Kinnaird played in every position in his nine FA Cup finals (including goalkeeper for Wanderers in 1877 when he conceded an own-goal). Kinnaird always wore white 'ducks' (trousers).

OLDHAM ATHLETIC AWAY 2008-9

Fluorescent yellow is not an attractive colour. It is acceptable, nay sensible, when worn by the emergency services and motorway maintenance engineers for reasons of health and safety. The Latics hardly fall into this category.

 © Offside

ORION 1887

In the nineteenth century the Scottish Football League was a closed shop dominated by the clubs from the densely populated central belt, leaving teams from the north and south of Scotland to compete in regional competitions. Orion were one of the stronger sides based in Aberdeen who were voluntarily wound up in 1903 along with the original Aberdeen FC and Victoria United in order to form the modern Aberdeen club and break into the Scottish League. Orion's original registered colours with the Scottish FA were 'Brunswick', a very dark green more usually associated with steam locomotives.

OUR BOYS 1877

The modern Dundee FC was formed in 1893 by the merger of two old clubs based in the city, both formed in 1877, East End FC and Our Boys FC. The latter team turned out in red and black adorned with caps until 1882, when they adopted rather more sober navy jerseys. It was these navy colours that Dundee adopted in 1901.

OXFORD UNITED 1987-9

Oxford switched from gold and black to yellow and blue in 1975, the blue turning to navy in 1985. All very good so far. However, their Umbro-designed shirts adopted in 1987 managed to combine three shades of yellow as well as white in a unique blend.

👉 www.classicfootballshirts.co.uk

PARTICK THISTLE 1994-5

Thistle are no strangers to brightly coloured strips, having adopted broad yellow and red hoops, trimmed in black, in January 1935 after borrowing a set from the West of Scotland rugby club. From 1975 vertical stripes were favoured and in 1994 these curious, blurred tricoloured shirts appeared.

👉 www.classicfootballshirts.co.uk

PARTICK THISTLE AWAY 2009-11

In 2008 Thistle took a gamble by introducing a novel away strip in pink and pale grey. After record-breaking replica sales, the management decided to introduce something even more outrageous the following season. The result was marketed as the first ever camouflage football shirt – an interesting concept since 'camouflage' normally allows the wearer to blend into the background, although it's hard to conceive just what environment this shirt would blend with. This outfit is proof that if you travel far enough in the direction of awful, you wind up in the realm of wonderful.

👉 Paul Paton poses proudly in Partick's preposterously patterned 2009 away kit. © Offside

PERTH GLORY AWAY 1996-8

Glory currently compete in the A-League, the top level of professional football in Australia. They are one of only three clubs that survived the collapse of the National Soccer League in 2004 after a government enquiry into mismanagement. They normally wear purple and white with orange trim but in the unlikely event of a colour clash, in 1996 they wore this grey and white outfit. The dramatic black splash now features as an integral element of the club crest.

www.oldfootballshirts.com

PETERBOROUGH UNITED AWAY 1993-4

There was a vogue for kits with extravagant paint-effects in the mid-1990s, typified by this example marketed under Peterborough's own Posh Leisure brand. The coloured streaks are overlaid onto a fabric imprinted with a complex jacquard pattern, demonstrating just how far the new dye sublimation print process could be taken. Rather like a novice magazine editor who has just discovered all those fancy fonts in his publishing software, the result is a mess.

www.oldfootballshirts.com

PLYMOUTH ARGYLE 1995-6

Argyle started to mess about with their traditional green shirts and white shorts in the 1960s. Mostly the results have been fine, often memorable, but this effort from 1995 pushed the boundaries just a little too far. There is really just too much going on. Since 2001 the club has returned to more traditional designs in their own unique Pantone shade of Argyle green.

☞ www.oldfootballshirts.com

RANGERS THIRD KIT 2007-8

Due to the sensitivities of Old Firm supporters, the colour palette for both Rangers' and Celtic's away strips is somewhat limited and both clubs now seek to distance themselves from the sectarianism that has disfigured their history. Rangers generally use variations of red, white and blue (although, controversially orange and blue, the colours of the Orange Order, have featured on two occasions) with occasional forays into other, neutral colour schemes. This example, in two shades of grey with light blue piping is a less than successful example.

☞ www.oldfootballshirts.com

READING 1991-2

☞ www.oldfootballshirts.com

During the 1980s, Reading faced serious financial problems and for a while a merger with Robert Maxwell's Oxford United to form a new club (Thames Valley Royals) was a serious possibility. They survived and in 1990 were bought by John Madejski, who set about rebuilding. Under Madejski's regime the sky blue, navy, white and amber colours adopted in 1983 were dropped but the beloved royal blue and white hoops did not make an immediate reappearance. Instead, these extraordinary shiny shirts with what can only be described as an interference pattern in navy were introduced. In the distance they appeared to be pale blue but at close range they could induce a migraine.

RED BULL SALZBURG 2010-11

Launched in 1987, sales of the carbonated drink Red Bull have catapulted its parent company into a multinational concern that has netted its two founders fortunes estimated to be in the region of $4 billion each. Red Bull GmbH is notable for its extremely aggressive approach to advertising and promotion, which includes the total immersion of the sports teams it owns in the brand: these currently include two Formula One racing teams, a NASCAR racing team, an Austrian hockey team and four football clubs.

When Red Bull bought the famous SV Austria Salzburg club in 2005, all traces of the past were erased including their traditional violet and white colours, replaced with Red Bull's red and white. They would now play in the Red Bull Arena and carry corporate branding on their shirts. This strip is included not so much because it is a bad design – in fact it's rather fine – but because it represents the total domination of global commerce over local sporting tradition. The three other football clubs owned by the company, Red Bull Brasil, Red Bull Leipzig and New York Red Bulls have all received similar treatment and wear identical strips.

As well as giving you wings, Red Bull brings you aggressive branding. © paphotos.com

REFEREES & LINESMEN 1940s

Match official W.E. Wood appears to have come straight from a walking holiday in the Lake District.
© paphotos.com

Until the end of the Second World War, match officials did not so much wear a kit as a suitable outfit for a vigorous weekend ramble. The referee in this wartime international between England and Scotland on 19 February 1944 is W.E. Wood. Disappointingly, despite the importance of the occasion, he is not wearing a tie.

ROYAL ALBERT 1886-9

In Scotland there is a long tradition of giving football clubs romantic, even fanciful names, perhaps by way of contrast to the grim industrial surroundings in which many of them were born. A good example is this club from Larkhall in South Lanarkshire, formed by the amalgamation of two colliery teams. The name comes not from the late consort of Queen Victoria but from the boat owned by the chairman who owned the pit. Albert briefly played in the ill-fated Scottish Third Division between 1923 and 1926 (in an altogether more suitable strip of black and white stripes, a good choice for a team with a mining heritage), going out of business a year later.

ROYAL ARTILLERY 1894-5

Royal Artillery FC were formed in the 1880s and played at the United Services ground in Burnaby Road, Portsmouth. The famous 'Pompey Chimes' sung by supporters of Portsmouth FC date from when the nearby Guildhall clock would strike out the quarter-hours and referees would time games to start and finish with the chimes.

Royal Artillery were a very successful and popular team in their day, playing in the Southern League and winning the Army Cup in 1898. They fell foul of the FA's rules on amateurism in 1899 for various misdemeanours, including the team having time off from duty to train and spending a few days at a spa hotel at the Army's expense. Following this the team dropped out of the Southern League and was disbanded shortly afterwards, paving the way for the modern professional Portsmouth FC to be formed to which many RA fans (and players) transferred their allegiance.

Unlike their more famous forebears, the Royal Engineers, Royal Artillery drew their players from the ranks. In keeping with Army tradition, the trainer was the Regimental Sergeant Major while the club secretary was, naturally, an officer.

The crest shown here is that of the Hampshire FA who regularly chose RA players. It was common practice at the time for players picked to represent their county FA or their country to sew the badges awarded on these occasions on to their club shirts.

ROYAL ENGINEERS 1872

The Sappers were credited with inventing the 'combination game' in the late 1860s, a style of play that required players to cooperate when most teams still relied on a single player to dribble upfield supported by a mob of team-mates. Royal Engineers were one of the leading sides in the era of gentleman-players and were beaten finalists in the first ever FA Cup final, when they played in this strip. While it looks very odd indeed by modern standards, it was fairly typical for its time. The dark red and blue colours are those of the Army while the cowls were a hangover from the days before uniform strips were introduced and teams were distinguished by wearing distinctive headgear, scarves or sashes. These gradually went out of fashion as more teams adopted uniform shirts and the novel skill of heading the ball made hats an unnecessary encumbrance.

SANTOS LAGUNA AWAY 2004–5

When shirt sponsorship was first permitted in England in the 1979/80 season (the Scottish FA had sanctioned the UK's first sponsorship deal by Hibs a year earlier), many regarded it as a step in the wrong direction, defacing the cherished shirts of favourite clubs. It did not take long before sponsorship became accepted and gradually the design of logos improved from the early plain text to become an integral element of the design. Secondary sponsorship is now permitted in the Football League and Scottish Leagues on the back of players' shirts as well as on the shorts. While this adds to the clutter of modern strips, the size and placement of logos is strictly regulated. This is not the case in some countries as this shirt worn by *Los Albiverdas* (the Green and Whites) in the top professional tier in Mexico demonstrates.

Whoever manages shirt sponsorship in Mexico has obviously never heard of the law of diminishing returns. www.oldfootballshirts.com

SCARBOROUGH 1929-31

For an old club (Scarborough were formed in 1879) it is surprising that no traditional colours were established before the team adopted red and white in 1961. Previously they changed colours with considerable abandon every few seasons, possibly because as a club of modest means, they played in whatever they could get hold of cheaply. This strip, worn in the Midland League, was just one of many extravagant outfits, featuring an enormous chevron that disappeared into the generous knickers of the period when the shirt was tucked in.

SCARBOROUGH 1997-8

It is easy to criticise the designers for producing naff strips but it is important to remember who makes the final decision.

'It is always the club that has the final word in choosing the kit design. We submit at least 10 to 12 different proposals each season and it is the club that picks the final one. Sometimes they pick something you were not expecting. In Scarborough's case, they were asking us for something "strange". The pattern was used for Genoa FC's away jersey in white, navy and red and was one of their supporters' favourites. Probably the change of colours did not give justice to the shirt! Sales were anyway good.'

FABRIZIO TADDEI, Errea Sportswear

☞ Errea

SCOTLAND AWAY 1995-6

 Chosen to offer an alternative to the wonderful tartan strip worn by the Scottish national side at Euro '96, the colours were taken from the tartan commissioned by the Scottish FA. Scotland did not progress beyond the group stage so this extravagant design was not seen in the tournament.

www.oldfootballshirts.com

 # SHEFFIELD UNITED 1990-2

Like most clubs who wore stripes, the Blades spent much of the 1990s reinventing their traditional designs for the leisurewear market. In the long run few of these attempts were successful and by the end of the decade they had fallen out of favour.

Shhh, Gazza, he might hear you and he looks ball-grabbingly annoyed. Even in that kit I wouldn't laugh at Vinnie Jones. © Offside

SHEFFIELD UNITED 1995-6

This shirt represents the extreme lengths United went to in the attempt to modernise their appearance in pursuit of the fashion fads of the time, and is probably the most controversial of all their tops. The narrow white stripes are fine, indeed have roots in the 'butcher's apron' stripes recorded as far back as 1890, but as for the rest? Oh dear.

SHEFFIELD WEDNESDAY AWAY 1986-7

In the interests of balance it is only fair that we examine Wednesday's back catalogue. Their home strips have remained broadly faithful to the tradition of royal blue and white stripes (albeit with an excursion into plain blue shirts with white sleeves in the 1960s, an outfit far too smart to appear here), but there were no inhibitions when it came to commissioning away strips. This shiny grey shirt with purple and white diagonal pinstripes was worn with purple shorts, a foretaste of far worse to come. Now a collector's item, you will get no change out of £100 to acquire one.

SHEFFIELD WEDNESDAY AWAY 1995-6

Almost a decade on and Wednesday went all out for the shell-suit and branded trainers market with this Puma offering in teal and something else with elaborate things going on in the horizontal bands. Good for wearing to the garden centre on Sunday morning with the pit bull in tow.

SHEFFIELD WEDNESDAY GOALKEEPER KIT 1993-4

 It may seem unfair to pick on Wednesday but this photograph of Kevin Pressman in the 1994 Coca Cola Cup semi-final sums up everything that went wrong with design in the 1990s. Busy, busy, busy.

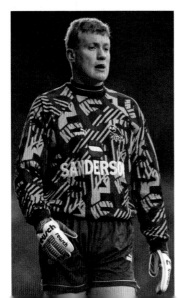

SHEFFIELD ZULUS 1879

The Zulus were formed to raise funds for widows and orphans of the Zulu War in South Africa. The members all played for clubs in the Sheffield area including The Wednesday. After two successful fixtures against a Sheffield Select XI, the Zulus toured Chesterfield, Derby, Nottingham and Barnsley, parading before each match in Zulu regalia. The players played under assumed Zulu names such as Umlathoosi, Cetewayo and Methlagazulu. In 1881 it emerged that the players had received payment for playing (professionalism was not permitted in England until 1885) and those found guilty were banned (leading to the abandonment of the Wharncliffe Charity Cup, an annual invitation tournament for leading teams in the city). The following year the Sheffield FA ordered the Zulus to disband.

SHIMIZU S-PULSE 1999-2000

They do rather like colourful kits in Japan and this spectacular outfit worn by the J-League 1 side from Shizuoka Prefecture is one of the most startling. The bright orange colour was chosen to celebrate the area's most famous product, the *mikan*, known in the west as the satsuma. The representation of a globe was a regular feature of their shirts around this time and was probably included to support their sponsorship by the Japanese national airline, JAL.

 © Offside www.classicfootballshirts.co.uk

SHOTTS IRONWORKS 1876-7

 Association Football was taken up by the working class in the west of Scotland somewhat earlier than in England. Most of the short-lived teams that sprang up adopted plain navy or maroon jerseys (or guernseys as they were often called); hard-wearing garments made from wool that were both cheap and readily available. The steel men of Shotts, however, opted for these splendid magenta tops for the single season that they were registered with the Scottish FA.

SHREWSBURY TOWN 1992-93

 This semi-abstract design would not look out of place on the wall of a second-year infants' class ('Jeremy's art and crafts has really come along this term') or as an entry for the Turner Prize. Appalling, dreadful and ludicrous are some of the more favourable adjectives applied to this particular shirt. Because the fabric was cut from larger bolts of cloth, each shirt is unique, so if you track one down, snap it up, frame it and hang it in the living room next to the Damien Hirst.

www.classicfootballshirts.co.uk

SOUTHAMPTON 1993-5

'The home kit of 1993–5 was Pony's first effort into the English market, from American Football to Premier League, the plan was to make the Pony 'tick' as big a brand worldwide as the Nike 'swoosh': the only thing they actually did was make Saints and West Ham laughing stocks of the football elite.

'The official unveiling of the kit saw Nicky Banger modelling the kit without a shirt sponsor, within weeks Dimplex's logo appeared and the shirt that had mixed reviews by fans was suddenly taken to the next level of grossness. However the kit appeared to go down a storm with supporters. A modern take on the traditional red and white stripes was what the fans wanted and got, the only real gripe was the fact that the away kit was identical in turquoise & royal blue: eye-catching to say the least (for all the wrong reasons). In these kits we also had to endure one of the

worst hate campaigns ever to hit the Dell, as well as the best action Matt Le Tissier ever produced in a Saints shirt, proving all his critics wrong. This kit, however wrong it appeared at the time, was donned by some great players and true Saints legends.'
GODFREY COOK, who worked in the Saints shop at the time

☞ Matt Le Tissier flogging a dead Pony. © Offside

SOUTHEND UNITED 1996-8

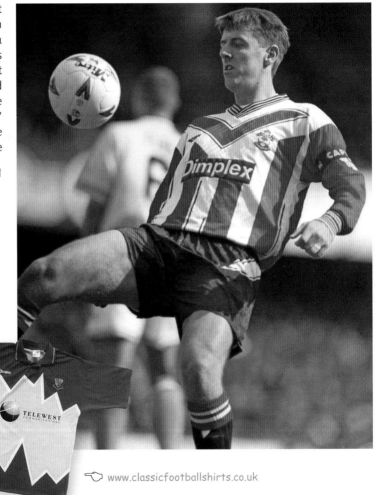

Throughout their history Southend have worn various shades of blue. Red was introduced as an accent colour in 1975 and in 1984 yellow became the secondary colour. This outfit from 1996 was the most spectacular of the blue and yellow strips, designed by Olympic Sports.

☞ www.classicfootballshirts.co.uk

SOUTHPORT 1995-6

In 1954 Southport FC, one of those northern clubs destined to eternal struggle, decided to replace their black and white stripes with the old gold and black strip they used as a change kit. Their fortunes did not improve but when Billy Bingham, the former Everton and Northern Ireland star, arrived as manager, things began to look up. First of all he had the team kitted out in all-old gold and then, in 1967, his 'golden boys' won promotion for the first time in their history. I know, because I was there.

In 1973 the 'Port won the Fourth Division but, somehow, the gold and blue worn at the time did not seem right. Decline followed and since 1978 the club has languished in non-league competition. This appalling orange and white thing was worn when Southport finished sixth in the Conference in 1996.

👉 www.oldfootballshirts.com

ST BERNARD'S 1878

Once upon a time St Bernards were a power in the land and could lay claim to being the third biggest club in Edinburgh. Formed as an offshoot of the 3rd Edinburgh Volunteer Rifle Corps by members who preferred football to part-time soldiering, the Saints were elected to the Scottish First Division in 1893 and won the Scottish FA Cup in 1895. They struggled to compete with Hearts and Hibs in the twentieth century, went into lengthy decline and were eventually wound up in 1943. Our graphic shows the teams' first colours, with St Bernard's Well, a local landmark, stitched onto their jerseys and a red scarf worn around the waist.

 ## ST JOHNSTONE 1994-6

Several clubs have sought to cash in on the boom in replica kit sales by marketing shirts under their own brand names but the economics of scale generally mean that the big global sportswear manufacturers squeeze these enterprises out. Here we have an effort by the Saints from Perth with a bizarre striped motif in various shades of blue.

👉 www.classicfootballshirts.co.uk

ST MIRREN 1901-7

Cream is an odd choice of colour and is rarely used – after all it clashes with white, one of the most common colours used in England and Scotland. Tottenham Hotspur's cashmere shirts worn in the 1920s tended to fade after many washes to a dirty cream colour but that does not really count. The Saints from Paisley, however, took to wearing this interesting shade at the beginning of the twentieth century.

ST MIRREN 1962-3

The Buddies' traditional strip is a black and white shirt worn with white shorts. That's striped *shirts* and plain white *shorts*. Black shorts are acceptable in short doses. Got that? Not too difficult is it? I am just trying to be very clear because in 1962 St Mirren's management seemed to have got confused. Newport County tried something similar ten years later and the players refused to wear their ludicrous orange and black stripy shorts after continuous catcalls from the fans.

STADE FRANÇAIS 2007-8

This is a bit of a cheat because this is in fact a professional Rugby Union team based in Paris. It is, however, hard to resist this wonderful shirt. Traditionally *Les Stadistes* have played in patriotic red, white and blue but since 2005 the club's president, Max Guazzini, a man known for his eccentricity as well as his nous for publicity has made a point of introducing extraordinary shirts each season. These have included a pink change strip, a design based on an Andy Warhol painting and this fabulous concoction featuring pink flowers and the fleur de lis.

☞ Matt Hall

STOCKPORT COUNTY 1913-14

After Bradford City won the FA Cup in 1911 wearing claret jerseys with an amber yoke, the design enjoyed a brief vogue among English and Scottish clubs. Stockport's flirtation with this style in salmon pink and claret was not a success and was dropped after one season in favour of blue and white stripes.

STOCKPORT COUNTY 1993-4

The shirt designed by Super League for Stockport in 1993 ranks among the very worst of the worst. Whatever you are looking for in a bad design you will find here. Incomprehensibly complicated hoops? Certainly sir. Jaggy lines in red and blue? No problem. Sponsor's logo rendered practically invisible? Absolutely. If your TV showed something like this you'd replace it.

 Stockport players express their joy at the sheer beauty of their 1993 home shirts. At least the goalkeeper's is fairly plain to offset the rather garish . . . oh no, wait. © Offside

 # STOKE CITY AWAY 1992-3

'Purple haze all in my brain
Lately things just don't seem the same
Actin' funny but I don't know why
'Scuse me while I kiss the sky'

JIMI HENDRIX

www.classicfootballshirts.co.uk

STRANRAER 1901-2

Before they settled on their familiar plain blue shirts and white shorts, the team from the famous Scottish ferry port played in all manner of colourful shirts. These orange and green tops came immediately after they had worn blue and green vertical stripes.

SWANSEA CITY 1995-6

Swansea have almost always worn all white. In the days before white socks became available, these were black. Orange trim was worn in the 1960s but was later replaced by black trimmings. In the 1990s red was added as an accent colour and the trimmings became more intrusive, as this example from Le Coq Sportif shows.

☞ www.classicfootballshirts.co.uk

SUNDERLAND 1981-3

Folk in the north-east of England are passionate about their football and deeply conservative about the strips worn by their clubs. When Sunderland adopted white shorts in an effort to revive their flagging fortunes in 1961, fans were unhappy. When Bob Stokoe restored their traditional black shorts on his appointment as manager in November 1972, his decision was greeted with general approval. This turned to rapture when his team beat Leeds in the 1973 FA Cup final. Imagine then the reaction when Le Coq Sportif redesigned the cherished strip with this concoction. Once their contract ran out, the French firm were shown the door and Nike arrived with an altogether more acceptable design.

☞ For some unfathomable reason, Le Coq Sportif's reinvention of Sunderland's traditional strip did not find much favour with the Mackems. © Offside

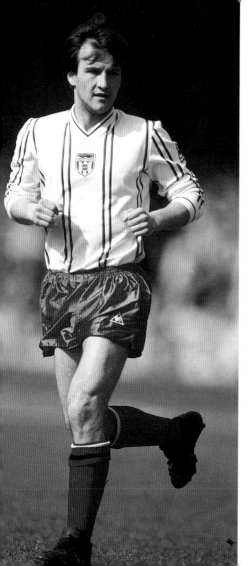

TORQUAY UNITED 1954–5

When a team has been in the doldrums for a long time, a change of colours is a way to make a fresh start. When success follows, as it did for Coventry City, Crystal Palace and the Brazilian national team, those behind the change are lauded as visionary heroes (as were Jimmy Hill, Terry Venables and Aldyr Garcia Schlee, the 19-year-old who designed the modern Brazil strip in 1954). On the other hand, failure results in derision. This was the dilemma confronted by Torquay United who had worn black and white since their formation in 1921 and had enjoyed a distinctly unimpressive career in the Football League. The new strip, adopted in 1954, was intended to evoke the golden sands and blue skies of the south-coast resort: the Magpies were transformed into the Gulls. There was nothing wrong with the new colours; indeed they were rather smart. The problem lay with the decision to have them made in a brand new shiny material, fancifully described as 'silk'. In fact they were made of rayon, a shiny artificial fabric first unveiled by Bolton Wanderers in the 1953 FA Cup final and which enjoyed a brief vogue over the next few years.

TOTTENHAM HOTSPUR AWAY 1991-2

'This kit was introduced as a third strip by Tottenham in the spring of 1992 and was worn for the first time in the home leg of the European Cup Winners' Cup quarter-final with Feyenoord. To be brutally honest, it was totally superfluous, as the existing yellow away kit would have easily sufficed. However, its use continued, occasionally as a first choice away kit, for the following two seasons.

'This was the third time light blue had been used by Spurs over the previous decade, initially with the superb Le Coq kit, but compared to that, this seemed utterly vulgar, as were most of the Spurs Umbro kits of the early 1990s, which were cluttered with bizarre patterns; but this was probably the worst culprit of them all. The idea that "SPURS" needed to be so blatantly emblazoned on the shirts and shorts seemed to be aimed at a market beyond those who knew what the cockerel on the shirt meant! This was the time of the start of the expansion and relaunch of top-flight football in the UK, with the introduction of the Premier League and Sky TV so, were the marketers encouraging new fans to "Pick your Team?" No, not a great kit and a worthy addition to this book.'

TONY SEALEY, Spurs fan and historian

☞ Just in case there was any doubt over identity, Tottenham's 1991 away shirt had 'Spurs' written across the chest. © Offside

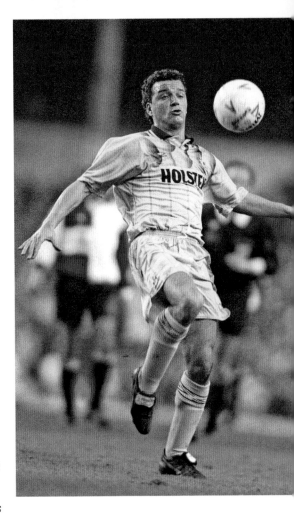

USA CHANGE KIT 1994

FIFA's decision to hold the 1994 World Cup in the United States, which at the time lacked a national professional league, was met with disbelief but there is no denying that the Americans know a thing or two about mounting a spectacle. The average attendances of 69,000 and an aggregate of almost 3.6 million for the tournament remain a record, despite the expansion of the final stages from 24 to 32 teams in 1998. The USA played in strips inspired by the national flag. First choice was wavy red and white stripes, evoking the rippling of the flag while the second choice, shown here, took stars as its motif, printed out of a curious denim-effect shirt.

☞ Alexei Lalas cuts a very fine figure in the USA's bizarre starry shirt. © Offside

VALE OF ATHOLL 1888–9

The Perthshire town of Pitlochry became a popular holiday destination after the railway arrived in 1863. It has no pretensions as a centre of Association Football but one of its modest teams, Vale of Atholl, which dates back to 1878, played for one season in breeches made from the local tartan. Now that is something I would like to see on a tin of shortbread.

ECRC VERANÓPOLIS 1997–8

'Being a self-confessed football club colour collecting nerd, any new strip discovered would be of interest and often excitement. However, this thrill could often be tempered by technical problems of my own making. As a designer, I enjoyed cataloguing each new addition by drawing the kit on a fairly small scale (this was necessary because of the ever-increasing size of my hobby), so detail was sometimes difficult.

'Usually, this was not an immense problem as most strips were fairly standard. However, some of the smaller clubs in the world, particularly those in the Brazilian state lower leagues, became very fanciful in their attitude towards design. Through various sources I came across many such clubs but was finally depressed on seeing the shirt of ECRC Veranópolis of Rio Grande do Sul. I knew previously, from being aware of the club badge, that there were lots of colours involved but on seeing the actual shirt pattern, I wondered if I had

☞ Bob Bickerton

pens fine enough to complete the illustration. The deceivingly plain yellow kit had a chest band design of white, red, yellow, green, blue, red and white 'diamond' – each interlocking with great precision and detail! Even with the finest of my pens I still required a magnifying glass to see what I was doing. I've always appreciated originality but my eyesight nearly went in the drawing of this strip – and for that reason alone I must name ECRC Veranópolis (c. 1997) as a choice of worst strip!'

BOB BICKERTON

WALES AWAY 1994-6

 'The first issue with this remarkable shirt was to identify the colour. Officially blue, it was also described as petrol blue, grey and even deep green. None of these has any connection with Wales' historical choice of alternate colours and Umbro take the blame for introducing a non-traditional colour, something Lotto and Kappa were later also guilty of. Why mess with tradition especially with a national team's colours?

'The style fell into Umbro's outlandish mid-1990s designs and was similar to their goalkeepers' and a Scotland away shirt of the era, but Wales had by far the worst colour combination. Worn in five outings, only one of which brought a win – a narrow home victory against those giants of world football, Moldova – it is not a shirt associated with success. Even more embarrassingly, it was worn in a World Cup warm-up game when Wales were beaten by Third Division Leyton Orient. A sad end to the six-year relationship with Umbro but worse was to come. . . .'

SIMON (SHAKEY) SHAKESHAFT, curator
www.walesmatchshirts.com

It's fair to say that Umbro's flirtation with abstract expressionism did not go down too well on the streets of Cardiff and Swansea. Simon Shakeshaft

WALES THIRD KIT 1996-7

'Officially this was styled as a lavishly decorated green third choice shirt. Shockingly garish, it looked like a leisure top that would not have been out of place on the golf course. With two shades of green, grading to white in places, pinstripes on part of the body, a geometric pattern across the middle and red detailing, this was one of the busiest shirts of the period. The first team wore it just once – a 6–4 defeat against Turkey, another reason fans disliked it. (Famously manager Bobby Gould tried to console the players by praising the fact they had scored four away from home. But they also conceded half-a-dozen, Bobby-bach.)

'The final straw was the ludicrous positioning of squad numbers squeezed under the national crest. When worn by the under-21 side, this was placed sensibly in the centre of the shirt.'

Simon Shakeshaft

SIMON (SHAKEY) SHAKESHAFT,
curator www.walesmatchshirts.com

WALSALL AWAY 1996-7

'You wouldn't necessarily have thought that the consequences of the break-up of Yugoslavia in the early 1990s would impact on the northern edge of the Black Country. However, the powers that be at Walsall FC were clearly monitoring the emergence of the Croatian national team and were struck by their unique shirt design (let's not mention Boavista). So, at the end of 1995/96 the club paraded the next season's playing kit and unveiled a stunning away shirt in a green and white chessboard pattern. Not that this was sufficiently extravagant – thin green lines ran down the shirt to ensure that the white squares were not plain. It was worn with green shorts and stockings, the socks oddly having a yellow and white hoop on the turnover. Although this kit lasted but one season it had clearly been a success as for 1997/98 the design was repeated in red and black for the home kit. The Saddlers' love affair with Eastern Europe (having also worn Poland's white-red-white and Hungary's red-white-green) has never been fully explained.'

NEIL MORRIS,
the only Walsall supporter in Ethiopia

WANDERERS 1872

Winners of the first FA Cup in 1872 wearing cerise, black and orange jerseys, Wanderers won the trophy another four times over the next six years. Without question one of the leading teams of gentlemen-players of the era, Wanderers drew their membership from the best former public school players. However, they went into decline as their players were drawn back to join one or more of the other ex-public school teams that sprang up in their wake. The club was wound up in 1887.

WATFORD 1898-9

In the late nineteenth century Watford had two professional teams, West Herts and Watford St Mary's. West Herts were also known as 'Watford' by die-hard members who had previously been supporters of Watford Rovers who had earlier merged with West Hertfordshire Rangers to form West Herts.

It soon became clear that the situation was unsustainable and the sensible solution was a merger of the two clubs. This came about in 1898 and the new team played in the Southern League wearing this wonderful combination, derived from West Herts' orange and yellow colours and those of Watford Rovers, which were olive and scarlet.

Straight from the ...ess-cot Stadium! Walsall ...dn't seem to mind being ...ddled' with this effort. ...w.oldfootballshirts.com

WATFORD 1928

Since the outbreak of the First World War in 1914, Watford had played in black and white stripes but in 1927, with financial problems looming large, management decided a new look was needed and dropped what was described at the time as their old 'semi-mourning' outfit in favour of blue shirts and white shorts. The following season, their colours were registered with the Football League as turquoise and white. Details of this unique combination have been extremely elusive (the club's records were destroyed in a fire many years ago) but based on the few scraps of evidence that have come to light, we can be reasonably confident of how the strip appeared. After a few seasons a more conventional blue was adopted but the mythology surrounding the turquoise shirts persisted with many reference books describing these as Watford's official colours right up until the late 1950s. In fact eyewitness accounts confirm that the team wore conventional blue after the war until gold and black was introduced in 1959.

WEST BROMWICH ALBION 1889

In their early years West Brom wore all sorts of colours, but in 1885 they settled on blue and white stripes. At the start of their second season in the Football League, these were dropped in favour of these scarlet and blue shirts with a stripe sewn into the side seam of the knickerbockers. Their fans hated the new look, dubbing the team 'Nigger Minstrels', a reference to a popular form of music hall entertainment. The new strip was quickly dropped and Albion reverted to blue and white.

WEST BROMWICH ALBION 1992-3

As we have already seen, reinterpreting striped shirts for the leisurewear market of the 1990s produced some truly nasty designs. West Brom's version of the barcode style included raggedy stripes that seemed calculated to increase business for opticians near the Hawthorns.

☞ www.oldfootballshirts.co.uk

WEST HAM UNITED 1991-2

American football was in vogue at the time so the Hammers decided to launch their own version. The short-sleeved version was okay but the long-sleeved ones were compared to pyjama tops. West Ham fans generally like to see their team wearing variations on the classic claret shirt with light blue sleeves but the club persists in launching mainly claret tops every couple of seasons. Perhaps it boosts sales when blue sleeves are brought back 'by popular demand'.

☞ Martin Allen in his PJs. © Offside

WHITEINCH 1874

The small working-class neighbourhood of Whiteinch lies a few miles west of Glasgow city centre on the north bank of the Clyde and until a few years ago was dominated by shipyards. The area is named after an island ('inch' is Scots for 'island') in the middle of the Clyde until it was dredged to allow for shipbuilding. Partick Thistle played in the area (twice) during their nomadic early history but local pride of place goes to long forgotten Whiteinch FC, who existed for just five seasons. Their otherwise plain navy jerseys were adorned with . . . wait for it . . . a one-inch stripe of white material.

WOLVERHAMPTON WANDERERS 1888-9

Before Wolves adopted their famous old gold and black colours in 1891, the team played in 'faded red and white stripes'. The strip shown here was worn in their first ever game in the Football League against Aston Villa and has various embellishments that did not appear in previous seasons, such as patches sewn into the shirts and an elaborate trim on the knickerbockers. No thought was given at the time to colour clashes. This became an issue when Wolves travelled to Sunderland in September 1890 and both teams turned out in nearly identical strips. This led the Football League to require teams to register their colours the following season and a rule was introduced that the home team should have a spare set of white tops available if the visitors' kit clashed.

WOLVERHAMPTON WANDERERS 1992-3

'Certainly one of the worst shirts to be produced by Wolves, this was either designed by someone who was very drunk or a West Brom fan. The tyre marks I suppose sound a good idea with the Goodyear sponsorship but this shirt should never hav got past a novelty drawing. The fact that it was made is of huge concern but I will always have some small affection for this shirt as it was the first ever Wolves top that I owned. I'm afraid that football shirts, particularly club home strips, must be traditional. Wolves play in gold shirts, black shorts and gold socks. I don't mind if the socks are the gold and black hoops from time to time, but that is as far as I will compromise. I never thought that this shirt could be beaten until Wolves brought out their new home shirt in 1996.'

PETER CRUMP, Wolves fan

☞ Steve Bull – Wolves legend. Alas this 'skid-mark' kit may be quite unforgettable but in quite a different way to Bull. © Offside

WOLVERHAMPTON WANDERERS 1996-7

Wolves' 1996 home shirt was designed around the shape of the wolf's head, rendered in gold on a black background. The wolf motif was repeated as a fading jacquard print on the body. For Peter Crump, 'This is the joint worst Wolves shirt of all time and there is no other way to describe it other than as an utter mess. I just hope the club sticks to traditional designs in future and we do not see any more like the two I've described.'

Not everyone agrees, however. David King says that, 'This is the best football shirt ever, well it's certainly the cleverest. The old gold part of the shirt is the Wolves' badge. Some fans hated the fact it moved away from tradition but I love it!'

☞ www.oldfootballshirts.com

YEOVIL TOWN 1997-8

The Italian sportswear company Errea have a reputation for producing excellent, bespoke designs for their clients and going out of their way to accommodate their wishes. Sometimes this can backfire.

'The pattern [we] used was based on one for Verona FC when they were in Serie A. I believe Yeovil looked to Italy for some inspiration that year. I was personally linked to this drawing because they [Yeovil, Scarborough and Middlesbrough] were the first English clubs I approached.'

FABRIZIO TADDEI, Errea Sportswear

☞ Errea

YORK CITY 1933-7

In the 1930s the main industries in the city of York were the railways and the manufacture of chocolate. The Rowntree family had established its confectionary business there in the nineteenth century and became, over time, one of the city's main employers. It was this association that prompted the York City board to switch from their traditional maroon jerseys to something a bit more, well, chocolatey. These novel shirts were replaced by more conventional red ones after five seasons. The official reason given at the time was to reduce the number of times the team had to change because of colour clashes with opponents.

YORK CITY 1974-5

After the conformity of the 1960s, clubs began to seek a little more individuality and the bright folk in York hit upon the idea of wearing a big, bold 'Y' on the front of the team's shirts. This maroon top was the home kit and was complemented by a white version that became the home strip the following season. Remembered now with considerable affection, it quickly became known as the 'Y-front', a reference to the ubiquitous male underpants of the period, available in a variety of colours. Younger readers may need to consult an adult over 50 for further information on this garment.

ACKNOWLEDGEMENTS

The author would like to thank www.classicfootballshirts.co.uk and www.oldfootballshirts.com for generously allowing the use of shirt images from their sites. Action photographs have been provided by Offside Sports Photography and paphotos.com.

Other images were provided by Birmingham City FC, Brighton & Hove Albion Collectors' and Historians' Society, Toffs (The Old Fashioned Football Shirt Company), Fraser Pettigrew, www.ambernectar.org, www.walesmatchshirts.com, Matt Hall and Bob Bickerton.

Details of the early kits of Scottish clubs researched by Alick Milne and Brian McColl.

Sketches are by the author assisted by Martin Latham.

A comprehensive graphic guide to the history of English and Scottish club kits can be found at www.historicalkits.co.uk.